Holy Transfiguration Monastery

The Monks of Mt. Tabor
(Byzantine-Ukrainian Catholic)

17001 Tomki Rd., Redwood Valley, CA 95470
(707) 485-8959

A Conversation with Paul

Wolfgang Trilling

A Conversation with Paul

CROSSROAD • NEW YORK

1987

The Crossroad Publishing Company
370 Lexington Avenue, New York, N.Y. 10017

Translated by John Bowden from the German
*Mit Paulus im Gespräch. Das Lebenswerk des grossen
Völkerapostels — eine Hinführung,*
published 1983 by Styria Verlag, Graz,
Vienna and Cologne 1983.

© Styria Verlag 1983

Translation © John Bowden 1986

Printed in the United States of America

Library of Congress Cataloging-in-Publication Data

Trilling, Wolfgang.
A conversation with Paul.

Translation of Mit Paulus im Gespräch.
1. Bible. N.T. Epistles of Paul—Criticism, interpretation, etc.   2. Paul, the Apostle, Saint.   I. Title.
BS2650.2T7413   1987   225.9'24   86-29207
ISBN 0-8245-0806-8

THE ARGUMENT OF THE BOOK

1

First of all we consider why it is that
Paul seems so 'alien' to us

2

Then we look for a standpoint from which the whole of his life,
his work and his unique thought (his theology) can be understood.
We find a divided life in which there is a 'before' and an 'after'

3

But this division goes right through the world situation in which
all human beings are involved, whether they were alive then,
are alive today or will be alive in the future

4

The change between an old world and a new one came about in
the man Jesus. But how can an individual become so significant
for everyone?

FOREWORD

I wonder whether anyone will read this book. That is a question I have sometimes asked myself while I have been writing it. Over the years even theological and religious books grow into mountains which make one reluctant to add yet one more item to the pile. And I have been deterred by some comments which I came across in passing: 'What do we have to do to make the most exciting book there is, the Bible, into the most boring of all books? Is it not enough that people use it for doctrines, sap its truths and make them into theologies? And that it has recently been reduced to the "kerygma"? But it is not meant to be used simply as a source or a quarry for the truths of faith. Certainly it contains these truths – but it is more: a living voice, a form of address, a call to people to repent, which demands new thinking and a change of direction, which is an incitement to unrest and an impulse for change.'[1] Still, I took the risk and went ahead, though it was really for a quite personal reason.

For a long time I have been concerned that the apostle Paul is so little known, indeed that he is intrinsically 'alien', especially to Catholics, like a closed park of which one can see something through the gate, but which one cannot enter and get to know. That observation led to my plan for a book like this. For a long time, too, I have wanted to pass on to others what I myself have come to know. Yet another reason was that for a long time there has been no book about Paul for Catholics which has introduced this man to readers with no theological training or little familiarity with theological literature, a Catholic equivalent of Guñther Bornkamm's splendid book for Protestants.[2] Things have changed very recently in Germany. There have been books about Paul by Heinrich Schlier, Eugen Walter, Eugen Biser and Josef Blank, to mention just those that I know about. However, I have not read any of them, although I could probably have learned a great deal from them.

I did not want to write a 'theology', a 'biography' of the apostle Paul, or even an 'introduction' to his writings and his work. I wanted to start a conversation with him and to introduce above all a Catholic readership to this conversation in the light of its traditions and sensibilities. So there are many topics which are not really discussed, gaps to which perhaps the professionals may point. There are hardly any notes and there is no bibliography. Nor is the book as a whole written in a systematic way or divided up into topics. I felt that it was much more important to listen and enter into the faith and thought of the apostle and to provide an introduction to it. That faith and thought is like a globe: no matter from what side you look at it, you see the whole thing from all sides. That applies to Paul, no matter how many hiatuses and unexplained probems there are in points of detail.

In a conversation, some things have to be recalled, repeated, expanded and seen in other connections. When writing it down, something which I have enjoyed very much despite all the interruptions, I have often been amazed and have thought: how much there is to be discovered, particularly for Catholic thought and belief and the Catholic way of life, and for our own situation, which has such a different character! Nevertheless, there has been much here that I could do no more than hint at.

In the English translation the texts have been quoted almost entirely from the Revised Standard Version.

I am particularly grateful to the Sisters in the old people's home at Seelingstädt bei Grimma in Saxony whose hospitality has contributed so much to the writing of this book, and I dedicate it to them in friendship.

I am also grateful to Styria Verlag and my friend the Director, Dr Gerhard Trenkler, for their commitment and the care they have taken over the printing.

Wolfgang Trilling

1 · First Impressions

To start the conversation off I would like to begin with a few personal recollections. Like most of us, I heard Paul for the first time in the readings at the Sunday service. He was part of the ordered and familiar course of events, the 'liturgy of the word', as we were later taught to say. By far the majority of the readings in the course of the church's year were taken from the letters of this man. How did that strike a young person of my age? What remained with me, what made an impression on me? Most of my feelings from that time have gone, and I can no longer remember them. But some things had a marked effect on me and stuck firmly in my memory.

On one occasion (and every year afterwards) there was talk of 'spirit' and 'flesh' and of an evidently irreconcilable battle between them, a battle which in fact takes place *in us*. Evidently each was concerned to defeat the other: 'For the desires of the flesh are against the Spirit, and the desires of the Spirit are against the flesh; for these are opposed to each other, to prevent you from doing what you would.' This sentence comes from a reading from the Letter to the Galatians (Gal.5.17). I found it quite exciting that something of this kind should be happening inside us – but I did not know what it meant, nor could anyone explain it to me (if a young person came up to me today and asked me about it, I would still probably begin to stutter). I found it exciting, as I did the passage about the armour of God which we all wanted to read out when we were young (Eph.6.10-17), because it described Christianity as something that needed courage and boldness, something for which we had to make an effort. But I did not understand what such an opposition of 'spirit' and 'flesh' might be.

1

The hymn of praise to love in I Corinthians 13 was an impressive reading. The text makes such a powerful impression because of its poetic and oratorical power and because of the totality of its statements:

> If I speak in the tongues of men and of angels,
> but have not love,
> I am a noisy gong or a clanging cymbal.
> And if I have prophetic powers,
> and understand all mysteries and all knowledge,
> and if I have all faith, so as to remove mountains,
> but have not love,
> I am nothing.
> If I give away all I have,
> and if I deliver my body to be burned,
> but have not love,
> I gain nothing.

That sounded like a great wind, like the breaking of enormous waves. And then it went on:

> Love is patient and kind;
> love is not arrogant or rude.
> Love does not insist on its own way;
> it is not irritable or resentful.
> It does not rejoice at wrong,
> but rejoices in the right.

That was clear and also seemed to be relevant. The 'great love' which was spoken of so resoundingly at the beginning is the same love that is created anew in ordinary everyday doings. It is not by nature a fantastic dream or a myth but a power which shows itself in numerous individual actions (as I came to think later). But then the passage goes on:

> Love bears all things,
> believes all things,
> hopes all things,
> endures all things.

How can that be possible, and is it right that it believes *all* things? Even lies, half-truths, meanness? Is not such talk very exaggerated, or is what it is about, love, so powerful that it can cope with even that? It took a long time, until I began to study theology, for me to begin to have any inkling how the apostle understood these remarks. But the hymn of praise to love was a glorious text for us. I wrote it out several times in calligraphy on parchment for friends from our group when they got married. I thought that if love was spoken of so strongly there, it must have something to do with marriage.

By far the most impressive thing of Paul's that I heard in church was the famous long reading (sacristans have always put it in that category) on what used to be one of the Sundays before Lent, Sexagesima. It was the passage in which the apostle says that he speaks like a fool, with a list of his adventures and sufferings. Today it is no longer read in context. It is the most powerful factor in producing something like a portrait of Paul.

How could anyone bear that? 'Often in danger of death'; then came the 'forty lashes less one', a phrase which one does not forget. The Jewish synagogues used forty less one, or thirty-nine, lashes to punish members who deviated in doctrine or offended in discipline.

And this happened five times to the apostate Paul:

Five times I have received at the hands of the Jews the forty lashes less one. Three times I have been beaten with rods; once I was stoned. Three times I have been shipwrecked; a night and a day I have been adrift at sea.

And then the catalogue of dangers:

In danger from rivers, danger from robbers, danger from my own people, danger from Gentiles, danger in the city, danger in the wilderness, danger at sea, danger from false brethren; in toil and hardship, through many a sleepless night, in hunger and thirst, often without food, in cold and exposure.

And finally his flight from Damascus: he escaped arrest by the police of the governor of King Aretas thanks to members of the community there who let him down the city wall in a basket – a

3

scene that we often find depicted in mediaeval pictures. The gates of the city were guarded.

But I was let down in a basket through a window in the wall, and escaped his hands.

What a life! And what greatness to be able to talk about it all as he does here! Not for empty showing-off and cheap self-commendation: that's the kind of man I am! It is in order to boast of the power which seems in fact to need his failure, his 'weakness'. After he had asked the Lord three times to be freed from a severe burden (it is mysteriously referred to as 'a thorn in the flesh' and 'a messenger of Satan'), he is told, 'My grace is sufficient for you, for my power is made perfect in weakness.' 'My grace' – that moves us deeply. Grace is clearly nothing thin, colourless or ethereal, no balsam for pious souls, but boundless power to bear and to overcome. So Paul has one last outburst. At the end of the oppressive series of sufferings there is an affirmation of these sufferings:

For the sake of Christ, then, I am content with weaknesses, insults, hardships, persecutions, and calamities, for when I am weak, then I am strong' (the whole text of this passage is in II Cor.11.16-12.10).

Even someone hearing or reading this for the first time will be affected by it. A few remarks of this kind are enough to draw our attention to a quite unusual, exposed, and passionate life, tempered with suffering, and to a personal testimony of the kind that we have from very few people. In those years there were only a few flashes, glimpses of the light. But the general context does not indicate that.

To this one could add the vivid description of the conversion of Saul/Paul which we find in Acts (three times, in fact, and slightly different each time). I myself certainly could not imagine – as so many people seem to today – that Paul himself did not describe his conversion experience in this way and never would have done, even if the event reads differently in his own writings (cf. Gal.1.15f.; I Cor.9.1; Phil.3.5-8): more restrained and yet more profound. His missionary journeys through half the Roman empire, ending with his martyr death in Rome, completed the biographical landmarks in the portrait of the apostle. It was all very imprecise, put together largely by chance, had a more emotional effect, touching the feelings, and not the intellectual impact that one might have expected from the teaching of the apostle to the nations.

Why is Paul alien to us?

It took a long time for me to begin to understand something of the teaching, the 'theology', of the apostle. Although we had eminent theologians and teachers during our studies, ultimately this area remained closed to me. However, we were constantly given the impression that the most important thing about the doctrine and the theology of Paul came into 'the doctrine of the church', as it was called. He had made his contribution to this, of course a very significant one, as an apostle, as a witness to the risen Jesus, as one of the first Christians and a man of the Spirit of God. One could pick all that up from him, indeed join him in reading it, since the main text of the 'doctrine of the church' had been written earlier. Even important New Testament lectures in which the apostle himself was presented without a filter and without the framework of a system could not alter the general impression given by my study of theology, that in this area I was involved with a systematic doctrine of the church.[3] The system indicates a context and incorporates the results of others. Non-theologians may also have had a similar impression. The doctrine of faith is not concerned with the individual voice; what is important is the overall result of 'what the church believes and presents as the faith'.

Why be concerned with the individual when we already have the whole? Even if we are dealing with someone of the status of an apostle, he is only one person and has only one voice in the choir. This deep-rooted basic 'Catholic' feeling, an idea of unity which is presupposed more than it is expressed, a feeling that tends increasingly strongly towards totality and harmony instead of going into individual details and differences, may itself already be the reason why Paul (the real Paul) seems to be 'alien' to the Catholic community. He is neither the type of a system – his theology is very unsystematic – nor is he a theologian of harmony. He himself has

5

no system (in the sense indicated here, of a closed structure of doctrine), nor does he fit into one. Since his time no one has succeeded in understanding him completely. There are kindred spirits who may have understood him profoundly because they thought in a similar way and because they had to reshape their lives after a break, like Aurelius Augustine, or Martin Luther. The Catholic predilection for thinking (and also for acting) in closed systems in which one already finds pat answers for all possible questions provides some immunity against the real Paul. The real Paul is someone who thinks in contradictions, in antitheses, which cannot be resolved at a higher level. Here is the bold pioneer of new, untried and sometimes indeed unsuccessful approaches. Here is the man of tradition, who adopts the basic insights of Christianity, but who, rather than quoting them word for word when he repeats them, develops them further in inexhaustible variants. He is someone who, like Odysseus, is 'much-travelled', who picks out and takes over much of what his world has to offer, from rabbinic Judaism, from Hellenistic views of religion, from Stoic philosophy, without levelling them all out in a system – a hard nut for subsequent theologians to crack when they attach so much importance to pure system. The real Paul is no fossilized lava flow but a volcano. He is not a cultured person who comfortably develops a clear doctrine or faith or even a 'Christian world view', but a focus of unrest, an unrest which can be compared with that felt by anyone who encounters the real Jesus in the Gospels. But systems do not value unrest; on the contrary, they cherish the tranquillity of clarity and order.

Paul is probably also alien because we know too little of what he wrote. That is really amazing when we think that in the New Testament alone we have thirteen letters bearing his name, far more than half the total number of letters in it, which amount to twenty-one in all, and roughly speaking form about a quarter of the New Testament. This external information leaves out of account the significance and the importance of Paul's letters. If we made an enquiry among Christians who played an active part in the life of their communities, to discover what even superficial knowledge of these letters they had, I fear that the result would not be a very favourable one. What letters do we have? In what situations were they written? What is their main content? Where do we find important insights and accounts intended for the life of the church (for example about the 'gifts of grace', about 'life in the Spirit', or the 'resurrection from the dead')?

In addition, there are quite a large number of letters in this Pauline collection (the Pauline corpus) which, while they bear Paul's name, were not actually written by him. These certainly comprise four of the thirteen letters (Ephesians, I Timothy, II Timothy and Titus) and with great probability two more (Colossians and II Thessalonians). Here we come upon the practice of 'pseud-epigraphy', in other words the composition of writings under the name of another authority: a widespread phenomenon in antiquity which can also be demonstrated within the New Testament collection. How that is to be explained and how one can come to terms with that as a Christian and a reader of scripture are questions with which theologians have been intensively preoccupied for years. This is a difficult area for all Christians who acknowledge the New Testament as the foundation of their faith. But it seems to me that it hits Catholic Christians particularly hard, since it is especially in such 'deutero-Pauline' letters that we find passages which are particularly close to the hearts of Catholics and which have been taken as characteristically Pauline. I am thinking of the opening of Colossians, the great hymn of praise to Christ, the head of all creation: 'He is the image of the invisible God, the firstborn of all creation; for in him all things were created, in heaven and on earth... all things were created through him and for him... He is the head of the body, the church... God sought to reconcile all things in heaven and on earth through Christ, who has made peace by the blood of his cross' (the whole text is in Col.1.15-20). Christ, the head of the body, his church – this great statement does not appear in Paul himself but it does appear in Colossians and in Ephesians and only there: 'And he has put all things under his feet and has made him the head over all things for the church, the fulness of him who fills all in all' (Eph.1.23).

The church, the mysterious body of Christ, was an idea which strongly stamped the generation after the First World War and led to a new experience of the church, an idea which also became the theme of an influential encyclical by Pope Pius XII (*Mystici Corporis Christi*, 1943).

Among the texts which are particularly familiar to Catholics I would also include the call to unity in the same letter (Eph.4.4-6), 'One body and one Spirit... one Lord, one faith, one baptism', and the interpretation of marriage as a mystery relating to Christ and the church (Eph.5.21-33). Both letters are important evidence of a developed theology and pastoral teaching from the Pauline school; the thought of both is bold and exalted, and they are full of a basic mood of praise and celebration. Catholic feelings about the faith find both confirmation and stimulation there (it is no coincidence that the two opening hymns in Col.1 and Eph.1 which I have already mentioned, with their universal christological horizon, have been included in the new Breviary, the book of offices for members of Orders and priests; I find this striking, not to say excessive). Finally, these images of the cosmic Christ of Col.1 and Eph.1 probably also prompted and led to the visions of Teilhard de Chardin.

Both letters probably also give sustenance and support to a basic Catholic temptation, to see the salvation prepared by God, achieved in Christ and communicated by the Holy Spirit as realized above all in the present, or, to put it rather better, to stress statements in scripture about the presence of this salvation so strongly that the other realization of salvation which is in the future, still to come, and only hoped for, fades into the background in such a way that the church is the form in which salvation is realized in the present. Both belong among the twenty-seven writings which the New Testament contains and which are therefore called canonical, i.e. normative, presenting binding 'doctrine'. But both are also to be read with an eye to other contrary statements in the New Testament which they supplement, and have to preserve their message from enthusiastic escapist consequences, perhaps even from the tendency to make Christianity an ideology.[4] Certainly the experience and viewpoint of the Catholic church has changed over the years, above all since the profound developments which have taken place in the wake of Vatican II. Much of the triumphalist idea of the church,

8

as it is called, has disappeared; indeed it was really already buried at the Council. I am just thinking of the many statements which were made there about the 'poverty' of the church and its 'service'. But old traditions are tough, and my impression is that at least in Europe we are still far from having been converted from such triumphalistic thinking. Nevertheless the mood towards the church has changed considerably. 'Behold this glorious house' does not fall so easily from the lips (if it is said at all), and instead there is often criticism, scepticism, even antipathy and disillusioned rejection.

Most New Testament scholars are now convinced that the Pastoral Epistles (I Timothy, II Timothy and Titus) do not come from Paul. These documents, too, were long seen as characteristically Catholic (early Catholic) and put as it were on the periphery of the New Testament. Their stress on 'ministry', tradition, church order, their elaboration of individual offices (bishop, presbyter, deacon), their firm and pragmatic sense of the opportunities for a Christianity which has to get organized for a long period in the world, their focus on right doctrine over against emergent heresies – all that already belongs to a church which is developing and thus differs markedly from the period when the communities were being founded through the impulse of the Spirit, the period to which Paul and the men of the first days of Christianity belong.

At this late stage the Pastorals also developed their picture of Paul and gave an impressive account of him. Many people will vividly recall a passage from II Timothy because it was read extremely often at feasts of church teachers, bishops and confessors:

I charge you in the presence of God and of Christ Jesus who is to judge the living and the dead, and by his appearing and his kingdom; preach the word, be urgent in season and out of season, convince, rebuke, and exhort, be unfailing in patience and in teaching. For the time is coming when people will not endure sound teaching, but having itching ears they will accumulate for themselves teachers to suit their own likings, and will turn away from listening to the truth and wander into myths. As for you, always be steady, endure suffering, do the work of an evangelist, fulfil your ministry. For I am already on the point of being sacrificed; the time of my departure has come. I have fought the good fight, I have finished the race, I have kept the faith. Henceforth there is laid up for me the crown of righteousness, which the Lord, the righteous judge, will award to me on that Day, and not only to me but also to all who have loved his appearing (II Tim.4.1-8).

This is an 'ecclesiastical' portrait of the apostle in the way in which it envisages others following in service and is meant to impress them: here is the trusty and true servant of the truth, and the witness of Christ, ready to suffer and experienced in suffering, the apostle and martyr. This is a portrait of Paul, but not Paul himself. So the quest for the real Paul is not so simple, and there also seem to be objective reasons why he is 'alien' to many people.

There is another point to make: if we asked people what they thought of Paul, as I mentioned above, it could turn out that the results among Protestant Christians were different from those among Catholics. There is a remarkable and sometimes curious division between the two princes of the apostles: Peter stands for (Roman) Catholic Christianity and Paul for Protestant Christianity; the one represents order and ministry, the other spirit and freedom. 'Petrine' thinking is therefore somewhat dubious, indeed alien, in the Protestant understanding of faith and thought about the church; just as theology and Christianity with a Pauline stamp are unusual and indeed really alien to Catholics. Now somewhere here there is also a grain of truth.

Certainly the fact that Martin Luther's great discovery of the liberating gospel was sparked off by a passage in Romans (1.17) plays a decisive role in the separate development of the confessions. And on the other side it may also be said that the famous passage in the Gospel of Matthew about Peter as the rock has been regarded as a key text for the confessional Roman Catholic understanding of the church in the period after the Reformation (Matt.16.17-19). I have noticed how many Catholic students of theology have no vital, committed relationship to Paul. I have also noted, conversely, that

Protestant theological students become intent and expectant over the exegesis of a particular saying of Paul's.

Considerations of this kind do not yet go very deep; in themselves they would not seem very disturbing. It seems to me that things become different when we get to a central Pauline theme, the theme of justification. Though I have no proof, I get the vague but instinctive feeling that most Catholics would not really be able to say what this expression of Paul's really means. If Catholics were asked whether they believed that the forgiveness of sins, 'sanctification' and a Christian life were given only by the grace of God and could in no way in the strict sense be earned by human beings, their reply would probably be: 'Yes, I believe that.' However, they would find it strange to call this justification, with a quite remarkable expression for this process, namely that God 'makes the sinner just', in other words that he saves the sinner, the lost one, radically by his 'grace' and into his grace. On the human side only 'faith' is needed and nothing else. That is the heart of Paul's teaching. That is the doctrine for the sake of which the Reformers formulated and resolutely defended their protest; moreover, it is a doctrine which for many Protestant Christians represents the authentic element in Christianity, and which is the distinctive characteristic of Paul's writings and of the New Testament. The word of the Bible is primarily the word of the justification of the sinner.

That also goes for some theologians who hold the view that the whole New Testament must be measured by the 'canon', by the criterion of the Pauline doctrine of justification and in accordance with it. This canon is not only indispensable – Protestant and Catholic Christians would agree on that – but there is also a 'canon in the canon', i.e. an inner standard for all the writings of the New Testament and what they say. Here Paul is made the measure of the New Testament, including the Gospels, Acts, the non-Pauline letters and Revelation.

Does not the danger of uniformity lurk here? Each of these twenty-seven writings speaks with different, distinctive words, of the one great thing that God has brought about in the 'fullness of time'. It is precisely this that constitutes the riches of the New

11

Testament. Each author of each writing is to praise God with his own voice. He must not transmit on the Pauline wavelength but has a wavelength of his own.

But above all there is one voice which has a particular place in the concert and an irreplaceable value, a voice which rings out powerfully through our Gospels, the voice of Jesus himself. Jesus has as it were the first word, and all the New Testament witnesses, even Paul, have the second. Much as Jesus and Paul are in agreement over quite essential matters, even on the question of 'pure grace' or 'grace alone', the difference between them must also be seen: Jesus has the basic word and Paul belongs among those who respond to it.[5]

Paul is not the filter and the standard for the New Testament. Nevertheless it may be that Catholics also feel less close to the apostle and particularly to his doctrine of justification because they have the impression that he represents Protestant Christianity more strongly and that the doctrine of justification is a typically Protestant affair. Lack of familiarity, inadequate knowledge, a failure to reflect on thought patterns that are taken over, or even prejudice, also serve in their way to produce strangeness.

Something else ought to be said here: Paul himself also shares the responsibility for this feeling that he is alien. There are two sides to him and he presents both sides naively, indeed sometimes unsparingly and abruptly. His character, his very personal way of feeling, reacting and thinking – all this also emerges. Paul is not a detached person and theologian, capable of expressing what moves him and what he has to say in balanced, measured, polished remarks. He is a passionate man and theologian who allows himself to be fully preoccupied and fully committed, indeed carried away, with whatever concerns him – and also tends to excess, towards both the good and the bad, in passionate love or in blazing anger. We find tones of the tenderest intimacy and sensitive tact alongside expressions of bitter sarcasm and unrestrained taunts. The feelings which Paul had towards the young community in Thessalonica were like those of a nurse, 'taking care of her children. So, being affectionately desirous of you, we were ready to share with you not only the gospel of God but also our own selves, because you had

12

become very dear to us' (I Thess.2.7f.). He is bereft of them 'in person not in heart' (I Thess.2.17). And the same warm and cordial tone can be found throughout the letter.

Yet there are passages of biting sharpness and harsh polemic, as in his verdicts on the 'opponents' in II Corinthians and also in Philippians (cf.e.g. II Cor.11.1-15; Phil.3.2). However much Paul is bothered about his objective concern, i.e. the purity and truth of 'the gospel', occasionally the bruised ego of the apostle seems to take over and to be confused with the word which should be serving the gospel. So the limitations within which we all live are particularly clear in Paul, because he wants utterly to bear witness to the gospel with body and soul, to be a servant of Jesus Christ.

It is always the whole man Paul whom we meet, lovable and even charming, and also arrogant, dominating and coarse, caught up in the vehemence of his theological visions and oppressed, bitterly oppressed, by disappointments and disasters of all kinds.

Paul also shows us two sides as a theologian. One side is charming, indeed enthusiastic, when he is talking about what is filling him to the brim, about the way in which he belongs to Christ and knows Christ. Just read passages like I Cor.4.7-18 or Phil.3.7-14. There his words pour out as if impelled by primal forces; there the way in which he puts things is so apt and impressive that it is impossible to forget them; his language breaks out of the usual patterns and finds imperishable modes of impression. Adolf Deissmann had a sense of this when he wrote:

'The letter killeth, the spirit giveth life' (II Cor.3.6): the man who had only written this monumental line would have been for its sake immortal.

'The Jews ask for signs and the Greeks seek after wisdom' (I Cor. 1.22);

'The kingdom of God is not in word but in power' (I Cor.4.20);

'Knowledge (Gnosis)puffs up, but love builds up' (I Cor.8.1);

'We know in part' (I Cor.13.9);

'The Spirit searches all things, yea, the deep things of God' (I Cor.2.10).

Such flashes and sparks come a hundred times in the letters, which were not intended for the applause of literary salons but came quietly and unassumingly to unknown people to help them in their need through power from above.[6]

And the other side? Anyone who has read one of the great letters attentively right through will have come across it. Here first of all we meet the rabbinic Jewish training which Paul underwent and which strongly marked his theological way of thinking, a style with which we are not familiar. We get some impression of this when we allow ourselves to be concerned with questions like, 'What shall we say then? Are we to continue in sin that grace may abound?' (Rom.6.1), or, 'What then? Are we to sin because we are not under law but under grace?' (Rom.6.15), or even, 'What shall we say then? That the law is sin?' (Rom.7.7). Or if we read argumentative texts like Rom.3.27-31 or Rom.7.1-6. This way of arguing and seeking to gain conviction sometimes seems to us to produce the opposite of what is intended. It sounds artificial, circumstantial, strained, and is often difficult or impossible to understand without elaborate explanations. No wonder that many people have given up here! No wonder, too, that people continually compare the simple, pictorial and impressive words of Jesus with it. How different the parables of Jesus are from these apparently stilted trains of thought! Paul does not make things simple for us, and it may have been the same during his lifetime.

Such impenetrable passages and protesting questions appear only where Paul is discussing with Jews or Jewish Christians – who may be really there or just imaginary. He seeks out the person with whom he is talking on that person's own level, thinks in his thought-patterns and fights with his weapons. However, the result of this is that we no longer have any clear idea of some of the points at issue between Pauline Christianity on the one hand and Judaism or a form of Jewish Christianity on the other,[7] that while we may get some intellectual grasp it is difficult to get on the same emotional wavelength. That applies particularly to the basic argument over the law (Mosaic – Old Testament – Jewish). What was at that time a matter of life and death is no longer a problem with which everything stands or falls – particularly because since then the problem has virtually been resolved. In my view that also holds for the churches of the Reformation and since the Reformation.

It is also often difficult to understand Paul because he uses terms to which he does not attach the meaning that we do. I have already indicated the difficulty of understanding the term 'flesh' as he means it. We shall have to mention that later. But the same is the case with many other terms, for example all the 'anthropological' terms like body, soul, spirit, heart, understanding, and above all terms like 'righteousness', which are so important for him. For him this really means the opposite to what we understand by it in everyday usage. Another quite unusual feature is the way in which he speaks of sin, death and even of the law in such a way that these seem to be personal powers which can provoke people, hold them captive, enslave them and overpower them.

How does one find a way into this kind of thinking? Or, to put it another way, where do we find parallels to it in our experience? A whole series of questions arises here.

Paul is also 'alien' for another reason, which must be mentioned in connection with what he thinks and says. He often follows tortuous courses over matters in which he is personally involved. There we have lines of argument which seem laborious and even tormented. All the freshness and openness that we notice elsewhere have disappeared. A tendency towards introversion seems to prevent us from understanding particular remarks simply and without reflection. Questions which are a matter of controversy between him and communities or groups of communities, or are simply 'under discussion', are drawn out at length with all kinds of assertions of honesty and good will; they are constantly stressed and then discussed all over again. Examples are the apostle's desire to pay a visit to the Corinthian community at a time when relations had become difficult (according to II Cor.1.15-2.4), questions about his financial expenditure and community finances generally, or the sense in which Paul may or must 'boast' (according to II Cor.10.12-12.13).

Here I would also include statements in which Paul speaks with an awareness of his apostolic authority and generally reflects on this aspect of his apostolic ministry. Sometimes one should assume that

15

the exercise of his authority – which was quite legitimate and usually recognized as such – was based on a self-awareness which had not been completely stabilized, and further that in practice it was not always obvious where boundaries were to be drawn. Where is he simply the voice of Christ and God and their authorized instrument? Where are we hearing the voice of the vulnerable Paul? One has only to listen to this passage from II Corinthians:

> Have you been thinking all along that we have been defending ourselves before you? It is in the sight of God that we have been speaking in Christ, and all for your upbuilding, beloved. For I fear that perhaps I may come and find you not what I wish, and that you may find me not what I wish; that perhaps there may be quarrelling, jealousy, anger, selfishness, slander, gossip, conceit, and disorder. I fear that when I come again my God may humble me before you, and I may have to mourn over many of those who sinned before and have not repented of the impurity, immorality, and licentiousness which they have practised (II Cor.12.19-21).

Who could say for sure that this was simply the voice of someone who had to speak in this way for the sake of his ministry and that this is not also the voice of the man Paul, sensitive, anxious, vulnerable, perhaps also in some ways uncertain?

I should perhaps also mention here a block which many people feel about Paul: Paul and women! A good deal could be said about this, but I shall limit myself here to the passage which above all has given him a bad reputation, namely his command that women must keep quiet in the community:

> As in all the churches of the saints, the women should keep silence in the churches. For they are not permitted to speak, but should be subordinate, as even the law says. If there is anything they desire to know, let them ask their husbands at home. For it is shameful for a woman to speak in church. What! Did the word of God originate with you, or are you the only ones it has reached? (I Cor.14.33b-36).

There is almost an irony here: scholars today are virtually

16

convinced that these particular words do not come from Paul himself but were inserted into the letter later. The most important indication of this is that in the same context, the ordering of worship at Corinth, Paul mentions the contribution of women with prophetic gifts as a matter of course (cf. I Cor.11.2-16).[8]

All this is part of the 'strangeness' of the apostle. I have done no more than give passing indications, evidence which must make us think. I wonder whether that is an encouragement or a deterrent to being concerned with Paul (again)?

I once 'discovered him', years ago. Since then I have not been able to forget him. However, sometimes I am attracted by him and sometimes he repels me. That happens even in the course of my study of, or comments on, the same letter. At one point I am enthusiastic about having discovered a pearl, and then I shake my head. But I cannot get rid of him, and in particular his contradictions are uniquely fascinating. I have the feeling that this will go on being the case. He is always disturbing, as he often has been in history. None of the first witnesses caused as much protest as he did.[9] And none has been as celebrated as he has been, down to the present day. An early voice, that of John Chrystostom, who died in 407, may stand as a representative:

Whenever I hear a reading from the letters of blessed Paul – twice, three times, indeed four times a week, when we celebrate the memory of the martyr – I rejoice in the sound of this spiritual trumpet. I become enthusiastic and feel a warm desire. When I hear his dear voice, I almost feel that I can see him in front of me and hear his explanations. But it oppresses and distresses me that not everyone knows this man as he deserves. Some people know so little of him that they do not even know how many letters he wrote. That is not because of a lack of intellectual capacity, but they fail to be concerned unceasingly with his writings. I too do not owe what I know – if I know anything – to a particular gift or insight, but I love this man and am constantly preoccupied with his writings. Anyone who loves a person knows more of him than anyone else, precisely because that person is important to him.[10]

2 · 'I have seen the Lord'

We shall begin with an extremely striking characteristic of Paul's language: his love of antithesis, i.e. of contrast and contrasting pairs. That happens time and time again: once – now; old man – new man; old covenant – new covenant; law – grace; darkness – light; letter – spirit; death – life; flesh – spirit, to mention only a few. There are people the structure of whose thought is such that they prefer contrast in formulating an idea. Some philosophers see the use of contrasts as the best or indeed the only possibility of talking about reality. In the secular rhetoric of the ancient world, its oratory and teaching, antithesis plays a prominent part, as it does in later Christian theology and preaching down the centuries. Antithesis is an impressive way of convincing people. It can also decline into cheap word-play. Paul had a gift for antithesis. A recent work on the subject gives a detailed account of the contrasts in Paul and draws this conclusion: 'The following list tells us a good deal about the actual breadth of the vocabulary of the contrasts in Paul. It shows that no thought of any importance whatsoever in Pauline theology is formulated other than in contrasts – or should one say, can be formulated in that way?'[11]

However, it is probably not only the structure of Paul's thought which produces this effect, and rhetorical skill which makes use of this impressive means. Both play a part, as is also the case with Augustine, but another factor in Paul is the experience of the fundamental divide in his life. The divide is the existential equivalent of the divide which has been brought about by God's action in Jesus Christ. This is an action which divides the times, which separates one period of history from another, an action which creates a 'before' and an 'after' and which makes all other distinctions of historical sequences and times unimportant, indeed ultimately does away with them. We shall have to discuss this later.

A divide runs through Paul's life; for him there is a 'before' and an 'after' which are in abrupt contrast, the first in utter darkness and the latter in clear light. That is the real antithesis which Paul discovers everywhere and brings to light, the antithesis which continually provides new nourishment for the structure of his thought. Because a divide runs through history there is also a divide through his life. And indeed conversely, in the divide which separates his life into two halves the apostle experiences in himself the great divide which runs through history. Paul does not fall victim to that kind of conversion mentality that does not allow any good points in one's own past and thus fails to do it justice. But God acts in him in the same revolutionary way in which he has largely acted within the history of humanity and for all human beings. No words are too great to express that:

Therefore, if anyone is in Christ, he is a new creation; the old has passed away, behold, the new has come' (II Cor. 5.17b).

'The old has passed away...' For Paul that is his own 'old' life, his life and thought as a Jew, as a Pharisee, as a persecutor of the young Christian community – a life which was as it were passionately focussed on God and concerned for his will. He led this life until the lightning struck him and burnt it all to ashes. Acts gives three descriptions of the so-called 'Damascus road experience', each time slightly different, depending on the context (cf. Acts 9.1-19a; 22.3-21; 26.2-23). These texts, and above all the first, shape our view and conception of Paul's experience. That is understandable (cf. the descriptions and pictures in old school Bibles) but it is a pity. For Paul himself often speaks of this decisive event; true, he does so in a restrained way and rarely, but also more directly and above all more authentically than is the case in the verbose and elaborate stories in Acts.

There we read in the first passage,

Now as he journeyed he approached Damascus, and suddenly a light from heaven flashed about him. And he fell to the ground and heard a voice saying to him, 'Saul, Saul, why do you persecute me?' And he said, 'Who are you, Lord?' And he said, 'I am Jesus, whom you are persecuting' (Acts 9.3-5).

The second description appears in a speech in which Paul is defending himself in the forecourt of the temple at Jerusalem. Paul explains: -

As I made my journey and drew near to Damascus, about noon a great light from heaven suddenly shone about me (Acts 22.6).

Then it goes on in the same words as the earlier passage.

The same thing happens a third time in a speech made by Paul before the governor Festus and King Agrippa in Caesarea (Acts 26.2-23). This time he reports an extended mission charge by the Lord who appears to him. Paul says:

At midday, O king, I saw on the way a light from heaven, brighter than the sun, shining around me and those who journeyed with me. And when we had all fallen to the ground, I heard a voice saying to me in the Hebrew language, 'Saul, Saul, why do you persecute me? It hurts you to kick against the goads.' And I said, 'Who are you, Lord?' And the Lord said, 'I am Jesus whom you are persecuting. But rise and stand upon your feet; for I have appeared to you for this purpose, to appoint you to serve and bear witness to the things in which you have seen me and to those in which I will appear to you, delivering you from the people and from the Gentiles – to whom I send you to open their eyes, that they may turn fom darkness to light and from the power of Satan to God, that they may receive forgiveness of sins and a place among those who are sanctified by faith in me' (Acts 26.13-18).

We cannot discuss the interesting differences and their significance here.[12] The main thing is that in all three narratives there is mention only of an appearance of *light* and then each time of a 'voice' which is recognizably the voice of Jesus. So there are two separate miraculous events, a light from heaven and a voice from heaven. But we do not have a clear indication of what Paul put in succinct form, 'Have I not seen the Lord?' (I Cor.9.1; but cf. the allusions in Acts 22.14, 17f. and in 9.17, 27; 26.16).

It is hard to imagine that Luke, who wrote Acts, was not aware that Paul himself claimed to have seen the Lord. This is the basis of Paul's credentials for the apostolate which were so challenged and which he defended so passionately. He is also convinced that he is the *last* of the witnesses to the risen Jesus who appears to him, as is also evident from I Cor.15.8f.:

> Last of all, as to one untimely born, he appeared also to me. For I am the least of the apostles, unfit to be called an apostle, because I persecuted the church of God.

Perhaps Luke wanted to avoid or tone down the impression that this was an Easter appearance of the Risen Lord, of the kind that happened to the witnesses who were called *before* Paul (cf. Luke 24.13-54: Acts 1.3-11).

Paul speaks in yet another passage, in Galatians (1.13-16), of the appearance of Christ to him. We must also combine a text in Philippians with this (3.4b-9). In both cases he sees his calling against the dark background of his former life. He was a Jew who strictly observed the law, indeed a Pharisee, filled with 'zeal' for everything Jewish. In addition, he tenaciously persecuted the community of Jesus. He is always aware of this aberration, indeed he even has to mention it in the list of witnesses to the appearances of the risen Christ (I Cor.15.5-9).

He was certainly not prepared for or disposed towards what surprised him and changed him. It came only from God, from God's goodness, and no human being had contributed to it. In the passage in Galatians Paul expresses this transforming experience in a different way from his account in I Corinthians. Whereas there he said that he had 'seen the Lord', now he says that God had revealed 'his Son' to him. Here is the whole text:

> For you have heard of my former life in Judaism, how I persecuted the church of God violently and tried to destroy it; but I advanced in Judaism beyond many of my own age among my people, so extremely zealous was I for the tradition of my fathers. But when

he who had set me apart before I was born, and had called me through his grace, was pleased to reveal his Son to me, in order that I might preach him among the Gentiles, I did not confer with flesh and blood (Gal.1.13-16).

Whereas in Galatians he has to defend himself against people who dispute whether he is a true and valid apostle, in Philippians he argues against others who set the community there at odds with one another by saying that Jewish circumcision is necessary even for Christians, and used it to bring up the question of the true nature of Judaism. Paul can also oblige with such Jewish 'values'. But they have become nothing to him, indeed they have become 'refuse' – as a result of the glittering new insight which came to him with Christ. That led to a 'revaluation of values'. What was gain to him is now loss, and what seemed to be loss is now gain; indeed all that happened earlier, and on which he built, has become utter rubbish, garbage. He uses a crude, vulgar expression.

Perhaps we should not understand it to indicate that Paul now casts aspersions on his past, since his life has been so changed. He probably means that in the light of the new foundation for his life which has been given him in Christ, his former life has become ridiculous and pitiful. How could he have thought that life important? It becomes incomprehensible to him afterwards, but only then. Nevertheless, it does sound remarkable when we hear someone dismissing the whole of his past, with everything that was once so important and so dear to him, as Paul does here. We shall only understand that when we have looked more closely at what the apostle means by 'his own righteousness' and a 'righteousness of faith' (cf. p.66). First let us listen to a text:

If any other man thinks he has reason for confidence in the flesh, I have more: circumcised on the eighth day, of the people of Israel, of the tribe of Benjamin, a Hebrew born of Hebrews; as to the law a Pharisee, as to zeal a persecutor of the church, as to righteousness under the law blameless. But whatever gain I had, I counted it loss for the sake of Christ. Indeed I count everything as loss because of the surpassing worth of knowing Christ Jesus my Lord. For his sake I have suffered the loss of all things, and count them as refuse, in order that I may gain Christ and be found in him, not having a righteousness of my own, based on law, but that which is through faith in Christ, the righteousness from God that depends on faith (Phil.3.4b-9).

'Knowing Christ Jesus' – that is what is overwhelmingly new. That is certainly first of all a reference to what he described in I Cor.9.1 as 'seeing the Lord'. This 'seeing' must have been so overwhelming that it transformed him at the same moment. He could 'know' the one whom he persecuted in his communities; he could see glowing with life the one who had been killed and whom he also wanted to kill in his communities. But 'knowing Christ Jesus' does not only mean knowing that the Jesus who was killed 'is alive'; it also means knowing that he is 'the Lord'. Paul not only recognized that Jesus lives, but also who he really is.

We must try to make clear to ourselves what it may mean that Paul's personal knowledge of Jesus derives from this event near Damascus. He did not know the 'earthly Jesus' from his own experience but only from what had been communicated to him. He was shown not the 'earthly Jesus' but the 'heavenly Christ'. Paul was not only given *faith* as to who this Jesus truly was, but he was also allowed to see him, to know him by sight. We must believe this Paul if we are to understand him. 'Have I not seen Jesus our Lord?' (I Cor.9.1).

The 'heavenly Christ' whom he saw was known to Paul as the Lord, the title by which he was called on and worshipped in the communities whom Paul persecuted. From this hour of grace onwards Jesus was also known to Paul as Lord. He became the one to whom Paul from now on intrinsically belonged, whom he loved, the being of his being: 'It is no longer I who live, but Christ who lives in me.' He became the one who took Paul into his service and did not let him go again, even when it became too much for Paul and he asked to be released:

And to keep me from being too elated by the abundance of revelations, a thorn was given me in the flesh, a messenger of Satan, to harass me, to keep me from being too elated. Three times I besought the Lord about this, that it should leave me;

but he said to me, 'My grace is sufficient for you, for my power is made perfect in weakness' (II Cor. 12.7-9a).[13]

Finally he became the one who had made Paul his 'apostle' and had given him authority. The supreme commission that a witness to Christ can have was also recognized by the Jerusalem authorities who had entered this service before him (Gal.2.9; cf. 2.1-10). And of course he was called and commissioned so that he preached the gospel, the Son, 'among the Gentiles' (Gal.1.16; cf. 1.1f.). Jesus – the Lord of Paul's being, the Lord of his way of life, the Lord of his apostolic service. There, with the Lord, all the threads come together. He is the new reality, which fills the new time.

Paul 'knows' Jesus, the Lord, by sight. He knows him as the glory (*doxa*) of Christ. On his face has shone the light that God once called from darkness at the beginning of creation and that now at the beginning of a new creation shines on the face of the new Adam. Paul was also allowed to 'know' a reflection of this light. He talks about it in an incomparable sentence in which we should probably see a reflection of the Damascus experience: 'For it is the God who said, "Let light shine out of darkness", who has shone in our hearts to give the light of the glory of God in the face of Jesus Christ' (II Cor.4.6).

Paul speaks of the glory of Christ as a glory which is also reflected from our 'veiled countenance': a bold idea which goes far beyond our 'normal' experience of faith but which might be accessible to Paul's own experience – I mean at the moment when Christ appeared to him.

And we all, with unveiled face, beholding the glory of the Lord, are being changed into his likeness from one degree of glory to another; for this comes from the Lord who is the Spirit (II Cor.3.18).

The knowledge of Jesus Christ – for Paul that is not something to learn, something that you get out of books, that is taught by a teacher, or that you can even learn yourself through study. This knowledge breaks into life; it affects the whole person and it also shines on his or her face. We need no longer have any fear that the

24

glory of God may blind or annihilate us as it did the children of Israel. Human beings can bear the gentle light of God which streams from Christ because in it Christ directs towards us the goodness of God that establishes and does not destroy; indeed it not only establishes, gives courage and confidence, but seeks to go even deeper: it seeks to change us into its own image, the image of Christ. To some people it may seem fantastic to apply this remark to oneself. I have spent just a while on Paul's remark and sought to make it clear that we have little inkling of where this man was taken in his 'knowledge' and what new worlds opened up to him. Perhaps we should spend more time on such passages and reflect on them more. The apostle is probably also referring to such insights when he says, 'The old has passed away, behold the new has come' (II Cor.5.17b). Do not such apparently adventurous thoughts transcend the harsh conditions of our present life as though it did not exist, as though we were already close to our goal, as though we were already completely new people? We shall see that Paul is well aware of this limit (pp.89ff.). However, such bold outbursts almost suggest that it was not there.

The 'Lord', the Kyrios whom he 'knows' because he has become known by him, is therefore also the 'Spirit-Lord', the Pneuma-Kyrios for him – a form of expression for the reality of the 'heavenly Christ'. Pneuma is the spirit and power of God, God's manner of being present among us, remaining utterly 'divine' and unconfused, and yet quite really there in our world. Not 'God with us' ('Immanuel'), one might say, but 'God among us and in us'. So for Paul, his Lord is not to be thought of as remote and enthroned far above the world but as being in the midst of the world, in the community, in the individual believer. Lord and Pneuma are identical. The Lord is a Pneuma-Kyrios who is and works as and in the Pneuma of God – and the Pneuma of God is at the same time simply the Pneuma of the Kyrios, and thus bound to a specific person, to Jesus, who died and rose again.

This idea of Paul's which is so hard to grasp also comes in II Corinthians. He has assured this community – since then theologians have puzzled over what he meant by his words – 'Now the Lord is the Spirit, and where the Spirit of the Lord is, there is freedom' (II Cor.3.17). Paul does not yet know the Pneuma, the Spirit of God, as a third divine person. This is a development in a later time. But what he says here – and in other places – about the Spirit of God belongs in meditation and reflection on the triune God and has not been superseded by subsequent speculations.

Spirit = Pneuma is a great theme in Paul. We must take up later the threads that we have discovered here.

Another key word for Paul occurs in the Philippians passage: righteousness:

> Not having a righteousness of my own, based on law, but that which is through faith in Christ, the righteousness from God that depends on faith (Phil 3.9b).

He had chosen a pattern of life and a form of life which was already available to him as a Jew – in the same way as most of us choose baptism – but which he seized on independently and sought to achieve it with utter devotion, to give a content to his life which was compressed into this one word, righteousness. It was to be a life which was to be utterly permeated by the will of God and tested by his commands, in daily service which would prove both hard and yet cheerful to both God and humanity. But God's will and instructions are contained in the law, the Torah of Moses. We should not deceive ourselves; that was a way which could arouse enthusiasm because it promised security and a certain goal. A sensitive person, attuned to a conscientious and righteous way of life, who was constantly attentive towards God and orientated on him, and also resolute enough in will, would find this pattern of life fascinating, as it was for example to the ethically demanding Pharisees. Paul was one of them. The watchword of this life-style was righteousness. Now, after the dawn of his new experience and many battles, Paul can call it, in a compressed and powerful way, 'my own righteousness (which comes) from the law'.

With Christ, that too changed fundamentally. With him there is a new righteousness which is not Paul's own because it comes 'from him', i.e. from his fulfilment of the law, 'from the law'. And there is a new way, namely faith in Christ. 'My own righteousness' in the former sense, Paul wants to say, could only come from me. But the new righteousness comes from God. That was the great liberating discovery which Paul made and which also belongs to the overwhelming knowledge of Jesus Christ. We shall attempt to see that even more clearly.

Here too Paul's antithetical language is evident. I shall contrast the pairs:

Righteousness

| my own righteousness from the law | righteousness from God (on the basis of faith) through faith in Christ |

and so on. I have spoken somewhat portentously of 'pattern of life', basis of life and form of life. However, we must see what Paul looks back on as a finished past in these comprehensive terms. That also applies to the new beginning with all its dynamics and future. The 'righteousness given from God' is not a single dowry, something like a present from godparents on the day of a baptism; it is the quality, the framework and the opportunities of the new pattern of life generally. The present already includes all the future in itself. The possession arouses further longing. The towering knowledge is there and is at the same time striven for further, also in connection with life in the new righteousness. Paul speaks of this in the same passage:

> That I may know Christ and the power of his resurrection, and may share his sufferings, becoming like him in his death, that if possible I may attain the resurrection from the dead. Not that I have already obtained this or am already perfect; but I press on to make it my own, because Christ Jesus has made me his own (Phil.3.10-12).

This passage is a good starting point for getting a first impression of what Paul means by righteousness, by justification, by law and faith (see further below, p.66), since here that is incorporated into his own experience, from which he speaks. And here – at the end of his career and his struggles – what sounds more complicated elsewhere is put in very simple and clear terms.

I said that Paul experienced in his own body, in his whole understanding of life, a period 'before' and a period 'after', before and after Damascus. For all the future left to him he could only think in this way. Here he gained an existential understanding of the fact that two fundamentally different situations had to be seen in everything, in history, in the course of the world. At one point the revolution took place, the transformation, an intervention of such force that it changed everything. And as in his own case, this was the intervention of God. This divine intervention took place in what we call the resurrection of Jesus. That was not only the earth-shaking happening in Jesus and for him, but the event which made a great divide through history and separated the old world from the new world now dawning. At any rate, that is how Paul saw things and shaped them in a pattern of Christian theology which first included all human beings and then the whole of creation and the world. How did he succeed in doing that?

He begins his thought with the resurrection of Jesus. There something unprecedented happened, which had never happened before, not even with Elijah, of whom the Old Testament said that he ascended into heaven in a chariot of fire (II Kings 1.11f.) and that he would come again before the end (Mal.3.23), nor even with Enoch, about whom there was an obscure sentence in the Old Testament saying that he was taken away to God (Gen.5.24). Here it was quite different, since Jesus had really died – indeed, as if to confirm that he had really died, his body had even been put in a grave, in other words buried in the usual way (cf. I Cor.15.4a). Death, to which all without exception fall victim, which holds fast its prey and does not surrender it, had in this one case to yield to the power of someone stronger, the power of God himself. But this one time was the decisive time.

Through that alone it has been demonstrated that death is not omnipotent (any longer) and that all without exception do not fall victim to it. What was possible and happened in one case can also happen in a second case, a third case, indeed in any number of cases. Certainly, for example in evolution, there are individual 'exceptions' or lucky chances which need not be repeated, although they could become extremely significant. But that does not hold for the strict logic with which Paul thinks: if it has proved possible at any time, even 'only' once, to overcome this giant called death who had been found invincible, then there is a power which can again defy him and conquer him.

However, in addition there is the decisive fact *who* it is who died and was raised from the dead. Such a revolutionary effect did not happen through just anyone. This was a quite special person, a person like no one else. Anyone who looks at the Gospels can see Jesus' concerns at every turn. No one spoke like him nor spoke such words as he did. He showed openly what moved him and yet ultimately remained unfathomable. Mysteriously he spoke of God and his rule (e.g. in the parables), and he remained impenetrable even to his fellow countrymen: quite simple, yet so difficult to understand.

The terms available to denote such men of God (e.g. righteous, prophet) fell short and did not match this experience: a unique nearness to God, something like 'God himself'. Paul had not experienced this searching and asking in previous years: Who is this man? He had only come to know the end of this course of questioning, which by the time he became a believer had resulted in an answer: this is the Christ (= Messiah), indeed he is Son of God. The way to that answer may even have been easier for Paul than for those who had known Jesus in his everyday life. But it pleased God to reveal to him 'his Son' (Gal.1.15f.), not the fellow countryman (cf. Mark 6.1-6a) nor even Jesus hanging on the cross. Here we are starting from the basis which existed for Paul and from which he continued to believe and think, without taking our questioning more deeply into its content and asking what 'Son of God' means and how we can understand it today. Paul knows it from a confessional text which he took over and which he also used to express his own faith. At the beginning of the letter to the Roman community, with which he was not personally acquainted, he assures his readers of this common basis in understanding what they both mean by gospel:

The gospel concerning his Son, who was descended from David according to the flesh and designated Son of God in power

29

according to the Spirit of holiness by his resurrection from the dead, Jesus Christ our Lord (Rom.1.3f.).

3 · Two Eras

The assertion that a human being had been 'raised' from the dead must have seemed alarming to Paul as a man of Jewish faith and as a Jewish theologian. For there is only a 'resurrection' when God's new world as a whole is dawning. And this would be the sure sign that the world which now exists is coming to an end. So if something like that had really happened, the tremendous conclusion to be drawn was that there was a change in eras or in worlds. Paul had not just noted that Jesus' resurrection was asserted by his followers. He himself had seen the dead one alive, in such an overwhelming way that he was certain that he had not been deceived or that the appearance had been merely a vision. And then he drew this consequence.

The idea of two world eras had developed in contemporary Judaism. One era, existing now, 'this age', is brought to an end by God's powerful intervention, by his judgment. Then the new age is created, which is also called 'the age to come', 'that age', 'the future age'. The two ages, eras, are in sharp contrast. The present one is governed by the powers of evil; the world to come will shine in clear light and in the consummation of the rule of God. The darker and more oppressive present conditions are felt to be, the more passionate the longing is for the pure world of God where distress is no more. In apocalyptic literature the situation of the dark present, the downfall of this era, with judgment on all the godless, the wicked, the enemies of the people of God, their punishment and the dawn of the era of glory is depicted in a dramatic way.

Behind this conception is a fundamentally pessimistic view of history in which the present world is no longer given any chance of

31

getting any better; it is a world which is doomed only to destruction. All hope is directed towards 'the beyond' of the other world, which only God can create. People can belong to that only if they are on the right side now. In addition the Qumran community, a kind of sect which separated from official Judaism and settled in the solitude of the Jordan valley, believed that the time of the end was so near that it also equipped itself in militant fashion for an imminent and decisive battle between the powers of evil and good. Paul's situation is to be understood against this background, which he knew from his past. He could have found it attractive to use this contrasting pair. On the other hand it also raised some problems. How did Paul cope with them? As we saw, his starting point is that the resurrection of Jesus has achieved the decisive breakthrough. The situation of the world has completely changed. The present era (this age) is no longer the same as it has been so far. Divine power has been introduced into it. It has really become a new era. Why only 'really'? We must look at that more closely.

To begin with, it must be pointed out that the most important thing for Paul is to find a way of saying that everything has changed in principle, and not just to describe the new existence of Jesus himself, the confirmation of his work and a way to freedom for believers, for the community and the church. No, 'the old has passed away, behold, the new has come' (II Cor.5.17) – and that applies not only for Christians but all along the line.

But in that case, we must ask, how can he maintain that? A *total* change, of the kind that should be expressed by the Jewish scheme of ages, has certainly not taken place. Seen from outside the world has remained the same. There are still catastrophes, violence, oppression, distresses of all kinds, and there is the denial of and fight against God and his people. And where can one experience the new world? Is it not crazy and fantastic to want to assert in all seriousness that everything has changed? Now so much is it the case that Paul has not thought through the change completely and drawn all the consequences (and they presumably did not even concern him), that we must suppose that he is making statements on very different levels.

First of all, he *never* said that the new age had already come;

32

indeed he does not use this common expression at all. Strong words are used to describe the new element, but it is never called the new age. So the new era has not dawned and begun in the way indicated by this Jewish expression. Therefore Paul refrains from using the terms to describe the new situation. That is an important observation. Had he used this form of expression the apostle would immediately have exposed himself to the incomprehending or aggressive questions of his Jewish opponents.

But another precaution which was necessary, given the situation of the Christian, also plays a role here. Such terminology could have supported or even provoked the view that people were already utterly in the new world, and were therefore completely outside the force of gravity, the seductiveness of the old. We must discuss later the danger of an enthusiastic 'resurrection theology' with which Paul was confronted. And in actual fact it had above all to be taken into account that the old era was 'somehow' still in existence. The only question is the sense in which this juxtaposition and intertwining of the two eras could be defined more exactly. Here too Paul found an amazingly bold answer (cf. p.81).

We must notice, though, that Paul *also* does not say that 'the old age' as such is ended, done away with, destroyed or replaced. All the occurrences of this expression indeed refer to the present, but they do so with different nuances. First of all there is mention in a more neutral sense of the pattern of periods: the waiting of the generation which wandered in the wilderness was 'written down for our instruction, upon whom the end of the ages has come' (I Cor.10.11). For Paul the existing age is also still 'evil' (cf. Gal.1.4), indeed dominated by the 'God of this world' ('this age', II Cor.4.4) and by the hostile 'rulers of this age', the authorities of this world, who are 'doomed to pass away' (I Cor.2.6; cf. 2.8). Paul sees not only that the enslaved powers of this world, sin and death have forfeited their position of unlimited domination, but also that yet other spiritual powers, the authorities of this world, are aggressively at work. This, too, is part of his world-view: the world-view of a man of antiquity.

The typical thought-patterns and patterns of behaviour which make this era evil and also continue to be dangerous for believers are also present and influential. Paul warns: 'Do not be conformed to this world but be transformed by the renewal of your mind' (Rom.12.2a). In addition to a wise man, a scribe, he also knows a 'debater of this age' (I Cor.1.20), people who advocate a 'wisdom of this world' (I Cor.2.6), a doctrine of the world and message of redemption which is in radical contradiction to the foolishness of God, which has now emerged as the true wisdom. In the language of the Johannine writings, that would be that one so-called wisdom is 'from below' and the other, real, one 'from above' (cf. John 8.23).

For Paul, too, 'this world' is coming to an end. Indeed he is so strongly under the impression that it will end *soon* that he expresses the conviction that he himself will belong among those who will meet the returning Lord during their lifetime (cf. I Cor.4.15,17: I Cor.15.51f.). The dead will be raised but those who are still alive will be caught up or changed (immediately, i.e. without the resurrection, ibid.).

But for him this era is not just ripe for destruction, since God's life is manifest in the midst of it. The new world has broken into the old world and has given it a new content. This distinguishes Paul fundamentally from the apocalyptic picture of history and its strict predetermination towards destruction. There are not just those saved from the end which is already heralded, as it were from the sinking ship, those who as the elect and the children of God will be preserved for a blessed future that is reserved for them. According to a difficult saying of Paul's, the whole creation is also 'subjected to futility', but at the same time is also endowed with a new hope:

> For the creation was subjected to futility, not of its own will but by the will of him who subjected it in hope; because the creation itself will be set free from its bondage in decay and obtain the glorious liberty of the children of God (Rom.8.20f.).

The authorities and rulers of this world are no rivals to God and the Lord Jesus Christ. They have power, but this is limited. They lose their influence where people live from the power that they are now already given by the Spirit of God. Every authority must now

– according to a hymn to Christ which Paul quotes – recognize the stature of the exalted Kyrios Jesus and 'bend the knee', 'everything in heaven, on earth and under the earth' (cf. Phil.2.5-11).

On the basis of his death and as a result of his resurrection Jesus has been exalted to become Lord and also exercises this Lordship. He is neither Lord 'in time' (but cf. I Cor.15.23-28) nor just Lord of his church. He is in truth the one Lord of all, alongside whom there is none other: '...yet for us there is one God, the Father, from whom are all things and for whom we exist, and one Lord, Jesus Christ, through whom are all things and through whom we exist' (I Cor.8.6).

What Paul seeks to understand from many aspects and to describe is an 'intermediate stage'. The new state of the world has really and irrefutably been introduced and established. But it is not yet completely realized. The dynamic of this intermediary situation cannot adequately be described with the favourite formula 'already – and not yet' any more than it can with the theological term 'a proleptic eschatology'.[14] For Paul the one is as true and as real as the other. Only rarely does he succeed in finding formulas in which both are said together (cf. Gal.5.25; cf. also Col.2.6).

The future dimension is retained, and with it hope or, to put it more accurately, faith as hope, in so far as it is also hope. But the future determines the present and the present can only be understood in terms of the future which is already at work in it. Listen to these words in which the future is also already promised as a possession:

> For all things are yours, whether Paul or Apollos or Cephas or the world or life or death or the present or the future, all are yours; and you are Christ's and Christ is God's (I Cor.3.21b-23).

But we must leave the most significant answer which Paul found for our intermediate situation between two worlds for a later time.

4 · An Old Adam and a New Adam

If we try to follow such far-reaching thoughts of Paul's and assess them, we may find them somewhat fraudulent. How can one draw such sweeping conclusions from a single event, which moreover is ultimately accessible only to faith, which has not taken place in a spectacular form before the eyes of the whole world like the appearance of Halley's comet? We believe that God is also constantly at work elsewhere and in a variety of ways, not just in this one place.

Here Paul is helped with a support, a support which proves so powerful that it can really bear the whole construction of this world-view. In the biblical Jewish tradition there is just one person who profoundly determined the fate of every single human being who followed him, and that is Adam, the first man. The whole of humanity – up to Christ – is Adamitic humanity, deriving from him, dependent on him, determined by him, grown together with him and in a sense identical with him: everyone is Adam and Adam is in everyone.

What if there were now another, new Adam? One who also became significant for all who followed and of decisive significance for their fate? And as his radical counterpart, a counter- and super-Adam? If the one stands for the fate of death and for a whole world under the sign of death and the other, new risen Adam stands for life and a whole world under this sign? This is in fact the course that Paul followed. Paul already found in Judaism the idea that the whole of humanity is represented in the one Adam, indeed really 'contained' in him as in a patriarch. He took it over and used it as a new basis for his universal world-view. But how did he develop it in detail?

The risen Christ stands at the beginning of a new time, just as Adam stood at the beginning of the old time. Paul contrasts the two and compares them, but only under one perspective: he asks what significance they have and what they did for the salvation of all other human beings, i.e. for the existence of humanity before God and for its deliverance. Here the first Adam is completely in the darkness. He is not seen as a 'patriarch of life', from whom humanity is physically descended – according to the biblical text and Jewish belief – but as the ancestor of death. Through his disobedience (his 'sin') death came into the world in accordance with the announcement, 'If you eat of the fruit of this tree you will die' (cf. Gen.2.17).

Adam opened the door through which two powers entered as usurpers and exercised their merciless rule: 'sin' (in the disobedience of Adam) and 'death' (as its consequence). Paul sees these as personal powers, superpowers, and he speaks of them as though they could decide and act like human individuals. Since Adam both are in the world and there is no one who can escape their grasp. All must sin as sons and daughters of such a father. This 'must' is not meant as an inner natural necessity nor caused by external compulsion. It is a kind of communal fate from which no one can escape, any more than he or she can escape from belonging to a clan, a people or a particular age. We do not make such associations; we find that they already exist and move within them.

However, there is something more than this pre-existing situation. One's own experience and scripture are confirmation that things are as they are, in other words that we all also in fact 'sin' as individuals (cf. Rom.3.9-18). 'All have sinned and fall short of the glory of God' (Rom.3.23) – that means the image of God which Adam had (and which now, far outshining the old, is illuminated on the face of Jesus Christ, the new man in the image of God; cf. II Cor.3.6). And all must die because they are sinners. Since Adam this curse and this fate has lain on them: as a collective person all are included in this one Adam. His action and fate are the action and fate of all humanity – up to Christ. Adam is treated as a superperson who includes within himself the whole of humanity like a mass of damnation. However, someone wanting to make things difficult could ask whether Abraham also belonged in this mass of damnation, as the apostle sees him in such a clear light, indeed as the type of the new righteousness by faith which comes with Christ (cf. Gal.3.6-29). Perhaps Paul would reject such a question. He thinks – though his thought is not easy for us to grasp – in representative figures: all who have a human face, as we have seen, are incorporated in Adam as sinners. But a new humanity is also already represented 'in' Abraham, a true Israel as God really intended it, a people which is founded on faith, like Abraham, and not on the law. Both hold for the apostle, are capable of proof and are convincingly demonstrated, even to those who have a Jewish background. It is not his way of thinking to set the two lines of argument over against each other or to play them off against each other. However, at all events it would be the case that Abraham too had to die, and therefore belongs in the age of death.[15]

But there is now another side to the parallel. Paul can also speak of Christ as a superperson and of a new humanity which belongs to him. For example we read:

But in fact Christ has been raised from the dead, the first fruits of those who have fallen asleep. For as by a man came death, by a man has come also the resurrection of the dead. For as in Adam all die, so also in Christ shall all be made alive (I Cor.15.20-22).

Or in the classical text:

Therefore as sin came into the world through one man and death through sin, and so death spread to all men because all men sinned (Rom.5.12);

and further:

Then as one man's trespass led to condemnation for all men, so one man's act of righteousness leads to acquittal and life for all men. For as by one man's disobedience many were made sinners, so by one man's obedience many will be made righteous (Rom.5.18,19).

So that, as sin reigned in death, grace also might reign through righteousness to eternal life through Jesus Christ our Lord (Rom.5.21).

If you read through the whole text of Rom.5.12-21 you can pick out the contrasts and compare them.

We may find it strange to think in the way that the apostle does. Perhaps we shall find a way into his thought by asking whether we do not also observe and experience something like spiritual powers which can develop a kind of life of their own. Death is perhaps the one with which we are most familiar. It has often been personified and depicted as a person, in paintings and in mediaeval and indeed modern mystery plays like *Everyman*. Hymns also express the conviction that death's omnipotence has been bestowed by someone who is stronger.

Cannot sin also become a power which, while it is built up of individual evil thoughts or actions, then develops a life of its own with an individual force of corruption which transcends the individual and establishes itself – and then goes on to seek out individuals and to destroy them? I am thinking of particular forms of advertising, the sex cult, and as it were atmospherically concentrated and omnipresent lies, contempt for human beings, the power of hate and images of the enemy (older people in my country will remember talk of the primeval enemy, France, the slogan 'God punish England', and so on). Today we have perhaps become particuarly sensitive to such major forms of sin which are built up from individual errors and guilty neglect, and then rebound terribly on their authors: the madness of re-armament, the devastation of nature, racial hatred, the rule of terror and other horrors.

Paul speaks of death and sin in the singular (he only mentions individual sins in particularly exceptional cases: Rom.7.5; I Cor.15.3; Gal.1.4; I Thess.2.16). That is straightforward terminology. Despite all the good things that may have happened in the time from Adam to Christ and did happen in it, as Paul himself knows, is ultimately and for a thoughtful approach a time of damnation and death. This world is a world of death.

It is also a world under the rule of sin. We must attempt briefly to understand what is meant by sin here. In the case of death that is not so necessary, although we must also look at that carefully too. First of all the pure fact of the physical dying of human beings is probably enough to understand it. But I shall have to show how Paul understands death even more radically than as an annihilation of existence generally (p.59).

However, on sin: we have only the one starting point, the disobedience of Adam, to indicate what the apostle understands by it. But if this one action could have had such consequences ('through sin death came into the world', cf. Rom.5.12; 6.23), then it cannot be a triviality, as is sometimes suggested by ridiculous popularizations of the biblical paradise story (a bite of the apple). The basic relationship between humanity (= Adam) and God must be affected. And we may look for this only in one direction: that human beings have departed from their role as creatures, been disobedient, put this basic relationship in question and terminated it. We could even risk saying that by cutting like a rope this vital tie by which it exists, humanity (= Adam) thus really gives itself over to death. Humanity dries up like a leaf fallen from a tree. And indeed we speak of the *fall*. This is not intended as some kind of stumbling from which it is easy to get up again, but as a fall into the abyss, from which we cannot free ourselves by our own efforts. By sin Paul is not so much thinking of individual failures, as we tend to, but more of a hopeless basic condition, an impossible situation – as in the case of the rider who cannot pull himself out of the mud by his hair and above all in the case of the powerful slave owner who enslaves and torments men and women. That is how dark the situation is which these two powers, death and sin, have produced.

But is this not a terribly pessimistic point of view? Everything black on black, without any shading? Especially as there is a further disastrous power to be added which has not yet been mentioned specifically: the law. For the law is seen as a power which makes demands and causes human beings even more misery (cf.I Cor.15.56). I would attempt to explain it like this: Paul is thinking in terms of Christ, in the light of the new age. There everything really is bright and good, far beyond all imagining, above all because

Paul knows that the omnipotence of the powers of sin and death has been broken. Generally speaking, and to begin with put in such sweeping terms, that is decisive. It produces such a clear light that seen in its brightness all the past, Adam's time, can only lie in deep darkness (Paul must also consider that there is not just pure light and pure darkness but also the grey between them, indeed grey for the present time in which all is not complete, but waits in hope, cf. Rom.8.24).

However, another observation must be made: the Adam-Christ parallel is not to be understood as if Christ only regained and brought back what had been lost with Adam – in some kind of paradisal state. No, the new situation is much more, and far exceeds the starting point with Adam. Here is no restoration of things as they were at the beginning – an idea which is in the history of religion – but a newness far in excess of the old, and that means the breakthrough and dawn of the End, the eschaton. For humanity in Christ the final future has already begun; in principle what has now been achieved will not be lost again. Paul expresses this 'more' on the side of Christ by contrasting *unequal* pairs in a complex argument. As a result of this, if we look at his argument closely, in some places it is obscure. His concern is to stress the otherness from the side of Christ in order to exclude the misunderstanding that what was lost has been restored, and above all to avoid the misunderstanding that Christ could be seen on the same level as Adam. So for example we read:

> But the free gift is not like the trespass. For if many died through one man's trespass, much more have the grace of God and the free gift in the grace of that one man Jesus Christ abounded for many. And the free gift is not like the effect of that one man's sin. For the judgment following one trespass brought condemnation, but the free gift following many trespasses brings justification (Rom.5.15f.).

Under the law

But Jesus of Nazareth now belongs in the old age. He was, as Paul puts it tersely, 'when the time had fully come... born of woman, born under the law' (Gal.4.4). Paul does not give biographical details, but two factors which are decisive for his thinking, which affect the whole of Jesus' existence: birth from a woman (so he is no heavenly being, demigod or the like) and the law. But the sentence goes on to give us the meaning of this being born under the law: 'and born under the law to redeem those who were under the law...'(Gal.4.4f.). So Jesus was put under the law for our sakes. Here we come up against that insight which has generally stamped the picture which Paul has of Jesus. It is a 'life for', from the first moment to the last breath.

As I have already indicated, Paul gives few specific details about the life of Jesus, says virtually nothing about Jesus' origins, his public activity, his healings, conflicts, travels, the calling of the disciples, the group of the Twelve, and also almost nothing – and this is even more strange – about the message of Jesus, about his great theme of the kingdom of God, the parables, everything that is collected in the Sermon on the Mount. We only find a few fragments of all this in the letters. That has always surprised people, and made them utterly amazed; especially when one thinks that Paul must have had adequate knowledge of this – since he lived such a short while afterwards and in view of the traditions about the Jesus event, which he must have come across everywhere in the communities. And may it not also be assumed with good reason that he himself had spoken about them and handed them down on his missionary journeys, in numerous sermons and in the first days of the new communities? In my view it is quite out of the question that he preached only in the way that his letters suggest. So why this silence about Jesus? In the last resort we can hardly decipher it, simply because we know too little about it.

We can think up a simple test in the opposite direction. If we try to imagine that for ten years Paul used only what we read in his letters as material in his addresses to larger and smaller audiences, his admonitions and instructions, his scriptural interpretation and his preaching of Christ, I think that it will become crystal clear that things do not add up. Can the experience that the apostle presupposes among the Galatian communities be the matter of listening to a mere statement, since nowhere in his writings do we

42

find details about the passion of Jesus? 'O foolish Galatians! Who has bewitched you, before whose eyes Jesus Christ was publicly portrayed as crucified?' (Gal.3.1).

Traces like this one in Gal.4.4f. need to be carefully investigated. Does not the apostle say a great deal when he understands the existence and career of Jesus as a 'life for'? That this passage in Galatians must in fact be interpreted in this way not only follows from it, but is also supported by many other things that the apostle says.

But first of all we must stay on the 'dark side'. That Jesus was subject to the law is a negative statement as far as Paul is concerned. Here too he is not interested in how Jesus was obligated to the law during his life, what demands it made, in what situations Jesus was required to observe the law, nor even – as we hear in the Gospels – whether and how Jesus got on in situations of conflict with the law or with the tradition of the scribes (cf. Mark 7.1-23). We know that Jesus' attitude to the law was characterized by sovereign freedom as well as natural acknowledgment. At least in one case Jesus even claimed to do away with an Old Testament regulation, namely the rules for divorce in Deut.24.1-4. Paul does not have such specific ideas when he speaks of the law in general terms.

He thinks overall of a disastrous power which in fact brings about the corruption of humanity. From the beginning the law is holy and the commandment is holy, just and good (Rom.7.12). Paul does not have the slightest doubt about that. But if the law comes from God it is given for life and belongs among the supreme possessions of the people (cf. Rom.9.4). For him, however, what is of decisive importance is the overall historical situation in which the law does its work. For this reason he sees an unprecedented change of circumstances coming about: in a situation generally dominated by the power of sin the law has not been able to achieve its original intention of leading to life and righteousness, but has been turned in the opposite direction. It has goaded on, provoked and activated the power of sin even more, so that its consequences are even worse than in the time without the law (i.e. before Moses). What was destined for life in fact becomes a power for death. Paul develops this theory in remarkable and difficult arguments, above all in Gal.2.16-3.25 and Rom.7.7-25. Right at the beginning we find these sentences which give some idea of his concern:

> What then shall we say? That the law is sin? By no means! Yet, if it had not been for the law, I should not have known sin. I should not have known what it is to covet if the law had not said, 'You shall not covet.' But sin, finding opportunity in the commandment, wrought in me all kinds of covetousness. Apart from the law sin lies dead. I was once alive apart from the law, but when the commandment came, sin revived and I died; the very commandment which promised life proved to be death to me (Rom.7.7-10).

So the decisive factor for the change in situation, for the reversal of the intention of the law, is the power of sin. If its backbone could be broken, could then the law again fulfil its original intention, of being the way to life? In fact this is the way in which the apostle sees things.

Paul never says that Jesus was so entangled in the law and the commandment that he was caught up in the same hopeless situation as other human beings under the law. Above all he never says that Jesus had sinned or had even been tempted to sin. On the contrary, we find in II Corinthians the words 'he who knew no sin' (5.21). The meaning of the phrase 'under the law' is to be found elsewhere: Jesus has to experience in his person the effects of such a life under the disastrous power of the law. He can say that it was life under a strict taskmaster, indeed a life in prison (Gal.3.23-25), painful and unfree.

Above all, however, it is an effect which Paul describes with a grisly expression, namely the word 'curse'. Life under the law is a cursed existence, like that of Sisyphus in the Greek saga, who has to roll a rock up a hill but never gets it to the top; or it is like the nightmare experience of being stuck in one place in a storm or a fire and despite every effort being unable to get away. It is a hopeless situation. People can strive for all they are worth but they are never able to fulfil the law as it should be fulfilled, wholly and perfectly. And so they constantly experience the other side of the same law, the threat of punishment, the verdict of guilty, the punishment

44

itself (read Old Testament legal texts like Ex.21.1-23.19; Deut.24;27 with this in mind). There is no way of getting out of the vicious circle, since there is no one who has fulfilled the law perfectly. Paul says this tersely and in a way which to Jewish ears is intolerable even today, but he never makes such a sharp statement elsewhere as he does in this passage:

> For all who rely on works of the law are under a curse; for it is written, 'Cursed be every one who does not abide by all things written in the book of the law, and do them' (Gal.3.10; cf. Deut.27.26).

The Son was sent into this existence. He did not sin, but he experienced the effects of sin in his body. The curse of such a sorry life was laid on him and he bore it. Paul recognizes this in the decisive event in which the essence of the life of Jesus is shown in its purity, in his death. 'Christ redeemed us from the curse of the law, having become a curse for us – for it is written: Cursed be every one who hangs on a tree' (Gal.3.13). How are we to understand that? Paul is thinking of the passage from scripture which applies to someone who has been executed and whose body is to be hung publicly outside the camp, the village, the city, on a tree, for all to see:

> And if a man has committed a crime punishable by death and he is put to death, and you hang him on a tree, his body shall not remain all night upon the tree, but you shall bury him the same day; for a hanged man is accursed by God; you shall not defile your land which the Lord your God gives you for an inheritance (Deut.21.22f.).

The scriptural saying was applied to the punishment of crucifixion which was used later. Anyone hung in this way on the cross is similarly cursed, because he dies a death of shame and dishonour.[16] Jesus died such a death. In this way it became evident that he bore this curse. Not because he had drawn it upon himself by his guilt but because he voluntarily accepted it for all those who were caught up in such an accursed existence. It was such a massive and weighty curse that Paul uses the unprecedented expression 'he became a curse for us'. He was as it were so completely absorbed or permeated by this curse that he became completely curse.

Since he did this 'for us', in our place, we are now free. 'But now we are discharged from the law, dead to that which held us captive, so that we serve not under the old written code but in the new life of the Spirit' (Rom.7.6). Paul first understands this in terms of the freedom to which we are called. 'For freedom Christ has set us free' (Gal.5.1a), and, 'For you were called to freedom, brothers' (Gal.5.13a). Law, the power of disaster, can now no longer affect us; it can make no further claim on us as the curse has been taken from this existence. For:

> Likewise, my brethren, you have died to the law through the body of Christ, so that you may belong to another... (Rom.7.4; cf. Gal.2.19).

Such concentrated remarks are perhaps only to be expected from someone who has had a similar experience, e.g. in conscription to military service in a meaningless war, compulsion to obey a 'law' in a situation which is clearly outside the law. The problems which the present situation of the world forces on us often do not disappear at all.

A statement which is as foolhardy and grim as that about the curse of the law appears in connection with another power, sin:

> For our sake he made him to be sin who knew no sin, so that in him we might become the righteousness of God (II Cor.5.21).

'Become curse', 'made sin': here too what was said above applies. The concentration of sin was laid upon him and he himself accepted it – again vicariously for us; indeed he was completely and utterly seized and poisoned by it so that he died of it. Sin killed him. That is once again shown by the ominous statement that death came through sin (cf. Rom.5.12a, above p.37), but then showed itself in the one who himself knew no sin. That is the last page in the book of Adamitic humanity, and this page is going to be turned right over. In actual fact one might think that the condemnation and execution of Jesus was a guilty, sinful event. He was given over into the hands of sinners (cf. Matt.26.45). But Paul sees more in this than a culpable individual act of the kind that happens every day, or even a judicial murder. For him the whole power of sin has concentrated itself at that particular point and raged yet again before itself receiving a fatal blow, before dying in the death of Jesus. There it now remains, even in death, like a dragon pierced with a spear. But for us the new chance of life emerged: having been freed from slavery under this power, we can now become the righteousness of God.

'He made him sin for us.' This statement raises another question. Certainly the positive orientation of what happened to Christ is already expressed in the 'for us'. But one may also ask how we can imagine a God who does such a thing, and does it to 'his Son'. Is it not cruel and heartless to hand him over and have him killed like this? Does God want or need such a 'sacrifice' for his wrath to be assuaged or his 'violated honour to be restored'? Such questions are always raised and sometimes also answered in the affirmative. But as far as Paul is concerned one has to answer them with a decisive 'no'. And that is true in two respects.

The first concerns talk about the 'wrath' of God. Paul uses the term above all in Romans and does so quite often (cf. Rom.1.18; 2.5; 3.5; 4.15; 5.9; 9.22; cf. also I Thess.1.10; 2.16; 5.9). Right at the beginning it sounds out like a trumpet:

> For the wrath of God is revealed from heaven against all ungodliness and wickedness of men who by their wickedness suppress the truth (Rom.1.18).

What is God's wrath? An emotion, an expression of feelings of rejection or even vengeance, or a stirring of his will? We can safely say that it is none of these but that 'wrath' is an expression for 'judgment', indeed for the final, last judgment. The day of judgment can also be called the 'day of wrath' (Rom.2.5). It is knowledge of judgment that ultimately makes human will and action responsible and binding.

'In Paul the wrath of God is not a divine emotion but a manifestation,' says Heinrich Schlier.[17] It is very important to remember that. Therefore no emotion of anger can be directed against the Son if he is loaded with the curse of the law and with sin. But life under the power of sin, in which sins are also committed in thousands of individual cases, stands under God's judgment. And the judgment, with the verdict and the inflicting of the penalty, in fact happens to the Son and in his death. Thus one can certainly follow the apostle in saying that in this death God judged sin and our sins and that he imposed the death penalty for them, but one may never say that God judged his Son or even wanted his death.

But we are to note another difference. At one point it is said that the Son himself became the curse of his own free choice, but at another that he was made sin, evidently by God. What is the relation between the two? Did God have some active effect on the cruel fate of his Son and was he himself involved in causing it? That is not an easy question to answer. However, perhaps a habit of Paul which we often come across will help us here. Sometimes he sees the whole event of our liberation and deliverance completely from God's side and expresses it as if it were only his concern. On the other hand he can also attribute the same event completely and utterly to the Son and call it his decision and his action. That is clear above all where Paul talks of love, the love of God and of the Son. There we also have the key word which gives us decisive help.

Paul is clearly not concerned with the subject of the individual statements, whether this is God or the Son of God; he seems to change them almost at random. The important thing is to say why this all happened, i.e. to indicate the direction, the purpose or the goal of the whole matter. The sense of direction emerges particularly clearly in these two passages, so that we can have no doubt at all as to what is meant. He became the curse so that we might be liberated by him; and God made him sin that we might become the righteousness of God. Nevertheless such a way of speaking sets us aback and shocks us deeply. We cannot neutralize it and tone it down, and it will always be offensive, in such a way as either to scandalize us or lead us to deeper insight.

Here we are at the most important point. Paul already has to hand the interpretation of the death of Jesus as a death 'for'; it is contained in the confession that he takes over, one of the oldest Christian compositions that we possess:

For I delivered to you as of first importance what I also received, that Christ died for our sins in accordance with the scriptures, that he was buried,
that he was raised on the third day in accordance with the scriptures,
and that he appeared to Cephas, then to the twelve (I Cor.15.3-5).

Here the 'for us' is interpreted in more detail as 'for our sins'. This 'for' is not to be taken in the sense of a compensation in substance, like balancing the weights of a pair of scales or calculating two values. This is not a business matter (not even a cultic piece of sacrificial business) but a personal event. The 'for' is the expression of the intervention of one for the other (who should really have made the contribution), the expression of an offer which is to apply to others as free gift, of the surrender of all that someone has and is, indeed even of the offering of a life. In a word, in Paul 'for' is an expression for an event of love.

First of all it is God's love which happens here, a love which can give completely: 'who was put to death for our trespasses and raised for our justification' (Rom.4.25). Or, in another way, 'But God shows his love for us in that while we were yet sinners Christ died for us' (Rom.5.8). This event of love also guarantees what will happen in the end: 'He who did not spare his own Son but gave him up for us all, will he not also give us all things with him' (Rom.8.32).

But the apostle also speaks similarly of the love of the Son, the love of Christ as his own free action and as the content of this 'for'. This whole life is impelled and given direction by this one power, love. Love is as it were the living principle of this life. It determines its existence as a 'life for' which is maintained and finally offered in a 'dying for'. That is what is said in a number of passages, as in Galatians. Paul wishes grace and peace from the Lord Jesus Christ, 'who gave himself for our sins' (Gal.1.4), and in the utterly personal formulation of faith 'in the Son of God who loved me and gave himself for me' (Gal.2.20). What is at work in his life becomes manifest in the surrender of this life (cf. also I Cor.8.11;

49

Rom.14.15). Here Paul has had a deep insight and made a decisive statement about the 'words and works' of Jesus, as they can also be read out of the Gospels. One thinks of Jesus' encounter with the 'woman who was a sinner', his action towards 'tax collectors and sinners', his concern for the sick, the weary and the heavy laden, of many of his words, the last meal in Jerusalem and his silent journey to death.

5 · God on the Gallows?

From the beginning it was clear that one cannot speak of the dying of Jesus, of his death, as a mere fact. That would be a possibility only if the first witnesses had wanted to express a particularly impressive, perhaps fearless and heroic, or patient and submissive, manner of dying. The story of the suffering of Jesus and his dying on Golgotha in fact does seems to be presented in this way. It was felt as being so significant and extraordinary that even the pagan commander of the execution squad in Mark says after Jesus' death, 'Truly, this was the Son of God' (Mark 15.39).

Often it is death which first demonstrates the ultimate motivation and content in a human life. It can happen that for the first time at death it becomes evident what power, concentration, boldness and also expectant openness are concealed in a human being, so that sometimes it takes death to make manifest what a person really was. In addition to many fearful, sudden and indeed tragic and incomprehensible deaths there are also instances in which a dying is 'successful', so that in it there comes to light once again something that had always been there, but which now is given a pure and undiluted form. One might think of the death of Jesus rather in this way, and the Gospels give us firm points of contact for so doing.

However, throughout the New Testament the death of Jesus is not mentioned because it is such a convincing dying, wholly focussed on God and nevertheless unerringly addressed to humanity. As we saw, it is expressed by Paul with the word obedience, as the opposite of the disobedience of 'Adam'. Here was someone who realized completely what Adam had failed to do and had refused to do, to say 'yes' to his role as a human being and thus a direct 'yes' to the holy will of the creator God. This 'obedience'

51

of Jesus shines out in the accounts in our Gospels right to the end, on the Mount of Olives. This death was not only exemplary, as in the case of any 'righteous' person, but it was also the cause of 'salvation'. Even this word 'salvation' is too pale and worn out for us, and communicates hardly any specific ideas to us. It is also a collective term. It is used in many significant remarks about our expectations of God which we ourselves are not in a position to spell out and for which we cannot hope; and not only our expectations, but also the 'good things' already promised by God, promised to us or already realized through his power and goodness. The biblical writings have a mass of expressions for these good things like peace, righteousness, blessing, life, deliverance. We already find them among the prophets of Israel and then of course throughout the New Testament. 'Salvation' is a comprehensive term for all of them.

Paul has a number of words and 'models' which help to make this death comprehensible. He already found some in existence, and some he probably discovered himself. They cannot all be cited and explained here. It is certain that they were close to the feelings of his time and probably some of them still strike home today, like the shocking expression, 'the cross'. In the religious Jewish literature of the time we find, for example, the fate of a 'righteous person' who is deeply involved in suffering ('humiliated') but is then 'exalted' by God; or the fate of the prophets whose voice is not heard, who are stifled by resistance and then murdered. The cultic sphere might provide the conception and terminology of a sacrifice, a sacrificial action in which 'the blood of Jesus' is shed and through which 'atonement' is achieved (cf. Rom.3.25, which is probably pre-Pauline). Yet this particular conception may have surprises in store for some who find it quite ordinary: 'At the periphery we have the fact that Paul never clearly described the death of Jesus as a sacrifice.'[18] He uses the term 'ransom' and the conception of a ransom of prisoners or even of slaves (cf. Gal.3.13); he speaks of liberation, redemption, deliverance, reconcilation and other things. Paul did not develop any of these many possibilities theologically on his own account; indeed he seems to have reservations about some of them.

Against this particular background his own choice to speak of the death of Jesus as the 'cross' makes a powerful impression. He uses this brief and concentrated expression to convey what can be said to clarify and interpret the significance of the death of Jesus. The word 'cross' manifests all the misery of the whole world and the incomprehensible descent of a truly divine love. We have already become long familiar with and accustomed to this word, perhaps all too familiar with it, so that it has lost its colour. When Paul made it the key to his understanding of the death of Jesus, those who heard it will have found it terrifying and gruesome. We can no longer sense what a presumption it must have seemed at that time to speak of God and his salvation with this word on one's lips and this image of the gallows before one's eyes. Paul was not only not ashamed to do this, but he also stressed most strongly that one *cannot* speak appropriately of the saving work of God without this word. For this is not a death which is regarded as praiseworthy and honourable, as people used to speak proudly of death 'on the battlefield' or 'for the fatherland', or of a sacrifice for others, for one's friends, for one's wife, forms of death which are regarded as ethically valuable and are recognized by public opinion. Paul feels that such instances are rare, as is indicated by the comparison which he produces:

Why, one will hardly die for a righteous man – though perhaps for a good man one will dare even to die. But God shows his love for us in that while we were yet sinners Christ died for us (Rom.5.7f.).

In the case of the dying of Jesus, no honour was to be gained and no reputation to be earned. On the contrary; there was a particular cruelty in this death penalty imposed in the grand style by the Romans, in that it was a shameful death; the victim was put on public display, tortured in a helpless state, surviving in pain often for hours and days and screaming in agony, exposed to the blazing sun or storms – that too was quite terrible. This penalty might not be imposed on Roman citizens. Above all slaves and rebels in the colonies experienced it. It was quite disgusting for those in antiquity with humane sensibilities, above all among the educated.

53

If we look all through the New Testament it is clear that this talk of the cross *in theological terms* appears only in Paul, with three echoes in non-Pauline letters, in Col.1.20; 2.14; Eph.2.16 (cf. Heb.12.2). The expression appears in the Gospels in the literal sense only in the passion narratives describing the crucifixion of Jesus (cf. also Rev.11.8) and also, in a transferred sense, in the saying about 'taking up the cross'. Only Paul uses 'the cross' as a theological expression. To talk in this way already indicates the contrariness, the foolishness of this expression. How can one 'talk of God' ('theology' means 'God-talk') in connection with this scandal? What believers see as the power and wisdom of God in the midst of weakness and folly, others can only see as a scandal and madness:

> But we preach Christ crucified, a stumbling-block to Jews and folly to Gentiles; but to those who are called, both Jews and Greeks, Christ the power of God and the wisdom of God (I Cor.1.23f.).

More than any other saying, this expresses the degree of helplessness which God incurred, the extremity and distress to which his love extended. There is no possibility of evading it, neutralizing it, toning it down, beautifying it. 'The cross' embodies the harshness, the contrariness and the mercilessness of the world which is left to itself and is not yet brought home to the love of God. That is 'the offence (the scandal) of the cross' (Gal.5.11) which is so important in Paul, for then and also for the present. At that time the love of God did not shatter on the resistance of hell but through it first reached its deepest, most powerful dimension – even to 'death on the cross' (Phil.2.8). We probably also have a new trace of it in the fact that this sign and the humiliation of God which it denotes is in solidarity with all who are humiliated and wounded, trampled down and exploited in our day,

Wherever the forces of destruction are still at work or have regained power, for example in a lapse into the old life of the 'old man' in Christ, there the cross is present. Anyone who fears and avoids the suffering which stems from belonging to Christ can be 'an enemy of the cross of Christ' (cf. Phil.3.18; Gal.6.12). Indeed

Paul can even talk of 'our old man' 'being crucified with' Christ, being crucified with Christ in baptism. There this old man 'dies'; now it is also to remain dead and not to revive again (cf. Rom.6.3-6; Gal.2.19). Thus the whole of the old world has been given a symbol in this sign, but this symbol has a foundation in bloody reality.

6 · Reflections on 'Resurrection'

So 'salvation' ultimately comes from the death of Jesus because this death is swallowed up in the victory of the resurrection. That was the experience at the beginning when the one who was believed in and had finally died showed himself to be alive, often and to many witnesses. Paul has taken over and kept for us the earliest list of these 'appearances' of the risen Jesus – invaluable evidence for the beginnings of Christianity (I Cor.15.5-7). Jesus had not remained dead, he did not need to remain alive only in the memory and the respect of his friends, those words that we so often hear and speak by the grave. He was actually alive in a quite new way through a unique and powerful act of God. 'God has raised him' now meant that what Jesus had begun had not died with him but went on; indeed once again it had a quite new beginning, in this power of God and with him, the living Lord. He has now truly become the Messiah = the Christ on whom Jewish expectation was focussed, the one who ushers in the end time (cf. Rom.1.4). Exalted to the right hand of God he now continues the work of God that he had begun and brings it to an end. This new reflection on him initially remained within the framework of Jewish conceptions and hopes for salvation. In Peter's speeches (and also those of Paul, as he is seen there) Acts gives an apt impression of this (for Peter cf. Acts 2.14-36; 3.11-26; 10.37-43; for Paul 13.16-41; 22.26f.).

Paul mentions twice in II Corinthians that he was in severe trouble which brought him close to death. The situation had seemed so hopeless to him that he had already written off his life, had already accepted his death sentence. His distress was so great that 'we despaired of life' (by 'we' Paul means himself). Anyone who has had to experience such hopelessness and the threat of death knows what Paul is talking about. We hear no more about what brought the apostle to such a desperate situaton. At all events he does not speak anywhere else so openly and so earnestly about any similar situation. The community is to know of this in order to be able to give thanks with him for his eventual deliverance. However, Paul had learned something in these straits which it was important for him to pass on: the power of God who raises the dead: 'Why, we felt that we had received the sentence of death; but that was to make us rely not on ourselves but on God who raises the dead' (II Cor.1.9; cf. the whole text 1.8-11). Paul means to say that he was already as good as dead, that he could add nothing more to his life, that he had to regard it as already finished. But the power of God reached even into this death. Because there is a God of whom one may also confess that 'he raises the dead'.

Those whose prayers are recorded in the Old Testament spoke with great confidence to God and used powerful comparisons: you are my rock (on which I can stand firmly), you are my fortress (in which I am secure), you are my shepherd (who constantly cares for me). Among them we find the idea that 'God kills and makes alive, takes down into the world of the dead and brings up again' (II Sam.2.6 etc.) and in the Jewish Eighteen Benedictions the phrase, 'Blessed are you, Yahweh, who makes the dead alive.' Belief that at the end there would be a real general resurrection from the dead had grown up in the two centuries before the time of Jesus. Paul had come to know it among the Pharisees and even argued it against the Sadducees, at least according to Acts (cf. 23.6; 24.15,21). Yet now the situation was completely changed. Paul is no longer concerned with a doctrine or even a principle of faith that he shared with the Pharisees; now it is the case that in one instance this has already happened. Not only will God raise everyone, but he has already raised one person. That is a new experience of God.

In his distress Paul has learned to pray to the God who raises the dead, because he raised Jesus. God is not only to be thought able to do such a thing; he has already done it. Even the distress of death and despair can be used by a God whose power is not at an end when faced with death. In the awareness of this experience it would be very foolish for Paul to want to put his trust in himself (II Cor.1.9).

Paul thinks completely in terms of God. It was through his overwhelming power that Jesus was raised (cf. I Cor.6.14). It is significant that Paul speaks only of God raising and being raised by God, and almost never of a rising of Jesus himself (the only exception being in I Thess.4.14). This statement 'he was raised' or 'he – God – raised him' (passive and active) occurs so often (twenty-two times!) that it must be regarded as a deliberate choice.[19] On the other hand we often, in fact seven times, find the noun 'resurrection' (of Jesus); the explanation of this may be that Paul is already using a terminology which has become established. But his own thought does not appear there, but rather where resurrection is understood as an act of God (just once it is the Spirit, the Pneuma, which raised Jesus from the dead, Rom.8.11). There his divinity, his divine sovereignty, is shown in a unique way – at any rate in our experience – in that he is wholly and incomparably God.

'Who raises the dead' can become a new divine predicate, a characterization which goes far beyond the traditional divine predicates like 'omniscient, omnipotent, all-gracious' and so on. Here there is a power for good which is not content with the state of the world (its deadly state), which confesses life and can even make life out of death. Paul also sees this power of God at work in the establishment of his own apostolate. Even in the opening greeting of the letter to the communities in Galatia he stresses this to indicate the authority behind that of his apostolate: he is 'an apostle – not from men nor through man, but through Jesus Christ and God the Father, who raised him from the dead' (Gal.1.1).

I assume that the event of the resurrection is also important for Paul as a demonstration of the power of God because it will be this power – and can only be this power – that will one day bring about a resurrection of humanity. Precisely this action is and remains reserved for God; in it his divine and sovereign power will be made manifest. As this has already happened once, the believer knows with the certainty that faith also gives him that this will happen for him again. 'God raised the Lord and will also raise us up by his power' (I Cor.6.14). 'He who raised the Lord Jesus will raise us also with Jesus and bring us with you into his presence' (II Cor.4.14). In associating the fate of Christians with that of Jesus Paul is arguing against people who deny the resurrection, an argument set out at length and dialectically in I Cor.15.12-19. However, we shall only grasp the logic which is at work there if we remember what has been said about the parallel between Adam and Christ (cf. above, pp.36-41).

But the apostle does not just direct his gaze and his hope towards the future. He also says that the believer can no longer ultimately be threatened by death. He says in jubilation that no power in the world, no threat, indeed not even death, can endanger the extent and grasp of the love of God (cf. Rom.8.38f.). Not even death! Of course all human beings, even Christians, must die their physical death. The community in Thessalonica which had to experience the death of some of its group was deeply confused. Paul comforted them by the assurance that their dead would be raised and would be taken up with Christ at his second coming (*parousia*, cf. I Thess.4.13-18).

However, he also recognized that not only will this physical death end later in a resurrection to life but it will not be a death of the whole person, death in the radical understanding as annihilation and total destruction. Behind that view of death is a biblical tradition which knows nothing of an immortality of the soul as a philosophical postulate. However, the one who lives 'after the flesh' will die in this complete sense: 'For if you live according to the flesh you will die, but if by the Spirit you put to death the deeds of the body you will live' (Rom.8.13). 'But then what return did you get from the things of which you are now ashamed? The end of those things is death' (Rom.6.21). The one who already lives 'in Christ' will be as it were supported and sustained through physical death. For death as a threat to one's own existence has lost its power. This death has already died in the death of Jesus. It can no longer destroy the one who is grasped by the love of God. The living power of the one who has been raised preserves this person through physical death. Victory may already be celebrated now, as Paul significantly writes at the end of his long explanation of (future) resurrection for the

Corinthian community: 'But thanks be to God, who gives us the victory through our Lord Jesus Christ' (I Cor.15.57).

Certainly such lofty ideas are not the sign of a presumptuous confidence which relies only on God's action and does nothing for itself. They do not conjure up any natural law to the effect that 'nothing else could happen'. Paul's intensive admonitions to maintain and work out what has been given to us tell decisively against that. But the believer is to be sure that there will be no withdrawal *on God's side*, that rather God is resolved to bring to completion what he has begun in us.

> He who did not spare his own Son but gave him up for us all, will he not also give us all things with him? (Rom.8.32; cf.8.30).

The resurrection of Jesus has from earliest times been the heart and the pride of the new faith. It embraces it all and as it were is a summary expression of it. The hope for the future which God has prepared and will bring about rests in the statement 'God has raised him from the dead'. The 'deliverance from the judgment (of wrath) to come' will happen through him 'whom he has raised from the dead'; as I Thessalonians puts it: '...to wait for his Son from heaven, whom he raised from the dead, Jesus who delivers us from the wrath to come' (1.10). A passage in Romans comes even nearer to being a short formula, a passage in which two confessions of faith elucidate each other. It is described as a 'word of faith' and seems to be quoted by the apostle as an already stereotyped formula:

> The word is near you, on your lips and in your heart (that is, the word of faith which we preach); because, if you confess with your lips that Jesus is the Lord and believe in your heart that God raised him from the dead, you will be saved. For man believes with his heart and so is justified, and he confesses with his lips and so is saved (Rom.10.8b-10).

Anyone who can speak like that and does so with inner conviction (with the heart) has said it all – that is what these texts mean.

To speak of a 'demonstration of power', indeed of God's power at all in this connection is very partisan: God uses his power for us, in our favour. It is a liberating, delivering, saving power, 'the power of salvation', one might say. I should stress again here that we have already found this in some remarks about the fate of Jesus. Just as it is possible to talk of Jesus living and dying for us, so too it is possible to talk of his being raised for us by God.

However, a danger arises with talk about resurrection, the danger that one could fall victim to the delusion that the resurrection of Jesus and faith in it already transposed the believer completely into the new world and raised him or her above the burdens and difficulties of daily life. Above all, some people thought that this final state had already been achieved through baptism. An enthusiastic faith misled them into believing that they had already transcended the harsh conditions of our life and were in a sphere of the spirit and freedom, even of arbitrariness and freedom, in moral life. This danger became acute in the community at Corinth, and Paul argues about it in sovereign and perceptive fashion in I Corinthians. Hence such a resurrection theology is also called the 'Corinthian danger' (cf. also Phil.3).

It continues to be a danger for the church to pass boldly over the reality of the world and its laws, to speak of a *consecratio mundi* (a consecration of the secular sphere, usually understood in sacramental terms) by the church or of recovering the world within the sacral sphere of God's salvation 'in the midst of this world'. Even those who devised and wrote the post-Vatican II prayers of the mass and the new Breviary may have had a slight tendency towards such a 'resurrection theology'.[20] The 'Corinthian danger' has not been banished once and for all.

In Corinth Paul countered this misunderstanding by setting the 'word of the cross' (cf. I Cor.1.18; 2.1) against it as sharply as possible. Our deliverance does not lie in a 'wisdom' which autonomously and arrogantly sets itself above earthly things, nor in a knowledge (*gnosis*) by which some people thought that they could judge and control everything from above. This is not, Paul says, the wisdom of God; it is not his knowledge, his spirit and his gift to us. This would be the worldly wisdom of human beings, self-made and falsely purporting to be the way to true knowledge; in reality it would be folly.

God's way ran in precisely the opposite direction: not towards the elevation and endorsement of someone who wanted to build himself up, liberate himself and develop his personality. God's way led to humiliation, to helplessness, even to shame, to the cross. And it was in this way that – paradoxically – his wisdom and his power and his spirit were shown. Without taking the cross into account and reflecting on it, it is illegitimate to think about resurrection. This remains the indispensable and indeed the infallible fact that characterizes God's real disposition – if we can use this word. Glory comes only out of humiliation and not without it – as with Jesus. That is also true of the proclamation of the message and those who bear it, of whom Paul himself is one (cf.I Cor.2.1-5). And he even reads it out of the composition of the community (its calling), although this need not be the 'law' of Christian communities for all times. There are not many wise in an earthly sense, not many powerful, not many prominent people. Paul presents this in strong words and powerful antitheses. Here is a long quotation from him:

> Has not God made foolish the wisdom of the world? For since, in the wisdom of God, the world did not know God through wisdom, it pleased God through the folly of what we preach to save those who believe. For Jews demand signs and Greeks seek wisdom, but we preach Christ crucified, a stumbling block to Jews and folly to Gentiles, but to those who are called, both Jews and Greeks, Christ the power of God and the wisdom of God. For the foolishness of God is wiser than men, and the weakness of God is stronger than men. For consider your call, brethren; not many of you were wise according to worldly standards, not many were powerful, not many were of noble birth; but God chose what is foolish in the world to shame the wise, God chose what is weak in the world to shame the strong, God chose what is low and despised in the world, even things that are not, to bring to nothing things that are, so that no human being might boast in the presence of God (I Cor.1.20b-29).

In the light of this experience it is understandable that Paul normally mentions the death and resurrection of Jesus together. Even where this does not happen explicitly, we must always bear in mind in the one case the presence of the other. That does not happen anywhere in the New Testament as consistently and as obviously as it does with him. The apostle can only see the two together as the basis of salvation. The one who was raised to divine life is always the one who also died for us, and the one who died is always the one who was so uniquely raised. Only when both are thought of together, in other words are indivisibly connected, can the dividing line between the old world and the new be grasped exactly.

I now want to indicate something else that is easy to overlook. Paul never speaks of the *cross* when he mentions the double event that brings salvation, but of the dying or death of Jesus. There is nowhere that he says, as we often do, 'cross and resurrection' or 'crucified and risen'. What may be the reason for that? First of all, it might be said that the apostle keeps to the stereotyped and traditional version: 'death and resurrection', 'dead and risen (or raised)' (cf.I Cor.15.3-5). However, that does not seem to be enough. It is also striking that the cross is mentioned only in polemical contexts where Paul is concerned to fight as fiercely as possible against views which relate to the substance, the distinctive character of being a Christian (and against those who put forward these views). That is the case with communities in Galatia, in Corinth and in Philippi. Only there, i.e. in Galatians (3.1; 5.11; 6.12,14), I Corinthians (1.13,17,18,23; 2.2,8) and Philippians (3.18) is there mention of the cross, and not in the long letter to the Romans,[21] in which the terms used are the dying or death and resurrection of Jesus.

Characteristically Pauline as it is, this talk of the cross is evidently an emphatic, radicalized terminology which Paul uses where danger threatens, where the whole of Christianity is at stake. Here he resorts to this extreme means because he is concerned that the cross of Christ should not be emptied, robbed of its power. He brands his enemies in Philippi, as we heard, 'enemies of the cross' (Phil.3.18) and understands his persecution by his opponents in Galatia as enmity 'because of the cross of Christ' (Gal.6.12). If he bowed to them and accepted circumcision as necessary for salvation,

63

then there would be peace between them and him, for in that case 'the scandal of the cross' would be removed (Gal.5.11).

So talk of the cross is not the 'normal' way of speaking of the death of Jesus and its saving effect, but an emphatic, polemical way. This observation leads to the question whether it is a good thing to use this Pauline expression so often and so naturally that its terrifying sharpness is no longer perceived. We might also ask whether it is really the case that a theology of the cross is the only legitimate Christian theology, indeed the Christian theology *par excellence*.[22] These words are also misused by 'pious' Christians, even by preachers and theologians, and misused through too frequent and easy or even rhetorical and bombastic usage. That could also make the word void, rob it of its force.

Paul speaks of the double event of 'death and resurrection' in a strict and concentrated dogmatic way. He gives none of the details about the circumstances of the suffering and dying of Jesus that are familiar to us from the Gospels and are even contained in the speeches in Acts. We get no information about historical details like the day, the hours (cf. the Gospel of Mark), the place of the crucifixion, names like those of Caiaphas or Pilate; and the role of leading Jewish groups is only hinted at. The same is true of the resurrection. Only in the tradition in I Cor.15.3-7 are we told that it happened on the third day and further what witnesses there were of the appearances of the Lord. But Paul does not speak in such detail anywhere else. That too may not be a coincidence. The only important thing for him is what he regards as the action of God and of Jesus and must be proclaimed as such in the strict sense. His thought is focussed in that direction and in this respect he is also a theologian (one who speaks of God) in the strict sense.

However, Paul does not use the word-pair 'dead and risen' in any stereotyped and formal way. The creative multiplicity and variety of his theological reflection is evident from the way in which it forms constantly new variants; indeed they evidently flood in on him when he speaks of this one thing. I cannot demonstrate that in detail here. In any case, it is fascinating to discover it for oneself.[23]

In my view the most significant passage comes – like so many of the apostle's deep insights – in II Corinthians:

For if we are beside ourselves, it is for God; if we are in our right mind, it is for you. For the love of Christ controls us, because we are convinced that one has died for all; therefore all have died. And he died for all, that those who live might live no longer for themselves but for him who for their sake died and was raised (II Cor.5.13-15; cf. also Rom.14.7-9; 15.3).

This text can be regarded as an 'existential' transformation of the confession which is handed down objectively in I Cor.15.3-5 and to which I have often referred. The 'for our sins' is significantly expanded into a universal 'for all' which embraces all human beings. And 'all' are already 'dead' in Jesus; they were – let us say potentially, in order to bridge a gap in understanding – freed from the miserable state of the old world in his death. And this dying 'for all' happened with a view to life, a life which was to be lived in accordance with its real meaning, and to a true fulfilment: not for oneself, egocentrically directed towards oneself and turned in on oneself and therefore always unfree, but 'for him', that is, for the new man Jesus Christ. In him the law of life 'for you' = 'for all' was at work even to the point of his death. I would also find a parallel in this great text to the earthly Jesus and to sayings like, 'Whoever seeks to gain his life will lose it, but whoever loses his life will preserve it' (Luke 17.3).

Paul has already taken over from Christian tradition the tendency to talk of the death and the resurrection of Jesus together, to see in both events the one fundamental saving act of God. But he has not only quoted, repeated this double formula but changed it and illuminated it in many ways. Constantly new aspects keep appearing to him. He draws many conclusions from it for the situation of the world as a whole and for our life in particular. We have discussed them in several contexts.

7 · What is the 'Righteousness of God' and 'Justification'?

But Paul is not just a thinker who penetrates to the depths of such remarks and brings their hidden content to light in a knowledge or wisdom directed by the Spirit (cf. I Cor.2.6-16). He is also a thinker who is concerned to speak of the activity of God in theological concepts and in this way to grasp its consequences for our understanding in faith. That is particularly necessary where there are opposing, competing interpretations or it is a matter of ruling out religious convictions and doctrines which at first sight are akin to Christian faith or may appear just capable of reconciliation with it.

However, there is only one view which the apostle thinks through and formulates with such sharp concepts. And this view is unfamiliar and strange to most of us. What I mean is the doctrine of the 'righteousness of God' and 'justification' which I mentioned briefly right at the beginning. In this case we must indeed speak of a doctrine, since Paul thought through this view, provided it with clear and sharp contours and developed it into a kind of system – it is probably the only instance of it in his case; otherwise he tended not to be concerned with the order and clarity of a doctrine. There must be strong reasons why here he does something unusual and resolutely keeps to it.

There is another remarkable thing. The righteousenss of God as a central doctrine of Paul's is really discussed only in Romans. The full expression 'righteousness of God' appears outside Romans only twice, in II Cor.5.21, an important passage which we have already got to know (p.46), and in a slightly different form, 'righteousness from God', in Phil.3.9 (cf. p.26). Of course that does not mean that the essence of what Paul describes as the righteousness of God is absent from his other letters. On the contrary, a careful look at the other texts shows that the basic conviction expressed with this remarkable term is present everywhere, even in the short letter to Philemon.

Nowhere, however, is it so central or expressed so conceptually in the apostle's 'theology' as in the letter to the Romans. The reason for this is that only in this work does Paul present 'his' gospel so comprehensively and so clearly. In all the other instances specific problems, dangers, needs, enquiries from the community are being discussed, and what the apostle says is governed by them. In Romans it is not easy to detect such a specific occasion for the theme and for the way the text is arranged. At first glance it seems to be quite general and independent of the situation and therefore to have been written without a specific purpose.

Why then did Paul write this letter at all, which seems more like a complicated tract than a letter to a community in a particular situation? We can only detect one situation with any certainty. Paul wants to prepare for his arrival among the Roman community by this lengthy letter. He had not founded this community, but regards it as part of his mission sphere and lying as it were within his competence as apostle to the Gentiles – in accordance with the agreement in Gal.2.7-9. So far he had not succeeded in visiting the community despite several attempts. Now, however, he sees an opportunity. He wants not only to go to Rome but also to seek the support and collaboration of the community for a missionary undertaking going even further west, as far as Spain (for this see Rom.1.8-15; 15.14-29). Paul introduces himself and his gospel to this community, which he does not yet know personally. At the same time he uses the occasion for drawing up a kind of summary of his insights, his proclamation over the years. Here is the mature fruit of his insight into, and experience of, faith, a unique document of the earliest Christian theology, complicated in detail and extremely compact, often difficult to understand, but always full of unprecedented insights and compelling formulas.

In this important treatise the righteousness of God plays a central role. So we shall keep to this text to see what the apostle means by it.

Right at the beginning the expression comes in a compressed formula, a sentence which takes the form of a definition and which at the same time represents the theme of the whole work. As was his custom, Paul had continued the address of his letter with a thanksgiving to God (Rom.1.8ff.), and in this recollective thanksgiving expressed his desire to visit the community and gain profit from a mutual exchange (1.11f.). He also felt under pressure to preach the good news, the gospel, to the community in Rome. This is what he has in view in writing the letter. As at the moment it is not yet possible for him to travel, though he hopes to be able to make the journey soon, he now explains in writing, in a concentrated argument, what the gospel has become for him, how he himself has been led to understand it and teach the content of this great word. It was certainly already a great word before the apostle encountered it among those who came to believe before him. For him it becomes a key word for the salvation of God which came into our world with Jesus:

> For I am not ashamed of the gospel: it is the power of God for salvation to everyone who has faith, to the Jew first and also to the Greek. For in it the righteousness of God is revealed through faith for faith; as it is written, 'He who through faith is righteous shall live' (Rom.1.16f.).

'Gospel' is not 'just' word, speech, message, 'good news', but is itself a power of God. A power comes with it and works through the word of the herald that comes from God and is itself divine. But 'power' does not mean just a demonstration of the overwhelming might of God towards man, the imposition of his stronger will or his superior ability through which we are perhaps more disturbed, forced into a corner, kept under and told firmly about our dependence, or anything of that sort. Many people originally expected that the end time would bring such a demonstration of divine power, a disclosure of the true state of things, a victory over all that was hostile to God through his well-considered intervention in the course of history: they expected judgment and terror. Paul also speaks of that in an impressive indictment which now follows (Rom.1.18-3.20); not, however, by painting a gloomy and frightening picture of a future judgment, as happens in apocalyptic literature, but by inexorably disclosing God's judgment already at work in the course of history, on Gentiles and Jews equally, by bringing out the previous history of humanity under the lordship of sin and thus under anger, i.e. under the indictment of God (cf. Rom.1.18). But this disclosure of the true state of humanity is not what first comes into his mind when he says 'gospel'.

Rather, the end time is ushered in by a clear call to freedom. The power of God is used for *deliverance*. The gospel is a 'power of God which saves everyone who believes' (Rom.1.16). It is no mere word that comes from the lips and penetrates the ears, which merely consists in the letter and appeals to the understanding – no, the urgent power of conviction and persuasion comes with the word. It seeks the centre of a person, the heart, and wants to command assent. It brings with it the supreme offer and the most promising prospect that we could be shown. That is expressed in the one word 'deliverance'.

It may not sound so vital and direct as the awareness of an existential lostness, and the longing to escape from this condition may not be felt so strongly as was the case with earlier generations. Analogies like that of a shipwreck on the high seas and a successful rescue at the last minute, or of a prisoner who is suddenly given freedom despite his realistic estimation of his hopeless position, no longer affect us deeply or strike a conscience aware of the need for deliverance. There are too many other strong, saving, helping, reassuring factors in our world of technology, of sovereign human ability: thousands of reassurances and assurances.

Yet Paul's use of the one word 'deliverance' denotes and leads us to consider all that he says about the relationships of power and domination in the world with or without the saving action of God; those we have discussed earlier. And these Pauline arguments which give us insight into and understanding of the true state of humanity may perhaps attune us more to what such a saving power could mean for us in such situations (shipwreck, imprisonment) – and thus illuminate the gospel that it brings.

The message of the gospel needs only one presupposition to be accepted and become effective, and that is faith. This already

69

appears again in v.16 and then in a more weighty form in v.17. At this point we can see the powerful break-through that the apostle's own experience and his years of reflection had achieved. The situation is one that we often find with significant discoveries, inventions or results of research. The end of a complicated and laborious process proves to be quite simple, almost natural; it is as though one could not have expected otherwise. That is also the case here.

This presupposition, 'faith', is the only one that is still needed; alongside it nothing else can be significant, like less or more education or even previous history and its contribution. Even the Jew who can refer back to a significant and splendid history has no advantage here over the man and woman from the pagan world. Granted, Paul says that this power of deliverance applies first to the Jews, but he then immediately adds 'but also to the Greeks' (= the Hellenes, here used for Gentiles, Rom.1.16).

The absolute presupposition of 'faith' therefore applies absolutely in so far as it is the only element which provides access to God's salvation. There is no other principle alongside it, indeed nothing at all which could provide such help or support. Of course that applies above all to the law, which does not come into consideration either as a precondition or as a concomitant factor of salvation in life. Precisely at this point Paul is rightly unyielding and consistent. Only faith is needed to achieve salvation and deliverance. No special prayers, rites of atonement, sacrifices with which God might be soothed or reconciled – as are called for in many religions – are needed here. Not even 'good works' which we perform ourselves and which we show to God as our achievement, and to direct his good pleasure towards us, are involved. That means that we do not have to build up any 'righteousness of our own', as Paul puts it (cf. Phil.3.9), which is then recognized by God and imputed to us as merit. No, in order to take part in and be assured of acceptance by God we need only the faith that he has done and does everything that brings about our deliverance.

That is an almost revolutionary insight which breaks through the systems of religions. It makes God completely and utterly God and gives him the supreme honour by attributing deliverance, what he alone can do and what cannot be done in any other way whatsoever by human beings on their own, to him alone without qualification. And it puts human beings in that position which is theirs as creatures, without oppressing them and keeping them under, namely by making responsive beings. The fact that human beings may give God a free 'yes' of assent and grateful acceptance gives them their value and their freedom. I find that amazing. And at the same time I regret that this doctrine 'by faith alone', with its solemnity and its effect on the knowledge of the essential nature of human beings, finds such little echo in normal Catholic consciousness.

On this last point in particular there is another important matter to be considered. Talk of 'faith alone' became suspect to our forebears because within the churches of the Reformation, too, it occasionally brought forth fruits which were not intended by the apostle, namely a low estimation of practical action, of proving oneself in life, of the acts of love, of ethics generally. 'Faith alone' could be so radicalized and exaggerated that the knowledge that this faith must also be worked out in life, indeed that only then does it show its authenticity, became blurred. It is hard to understand how this was possible with reference to Paul, since in countless passages he puts the strongest emphasis on the need to walk according to faith. The summons and admonition to this (called *paraenesis* or *paraklesis*) runs through all his letters, from I Thessalonians to Philippians and Philemon. I Corinthians is one such admonition almost from beginning to end, in which the individual themes discussed are illuminated and deepened theologically.

The Pauline formula 'faith alone' is closely focussed on the beginning of the receiving of salvation, on the beginning of being a Christian, on the basic answer to the message of the gospel. Here it is unrivalled; here no works of any kind have a role, not even openness and readiness for the divine call, repentance over previous life, the search for forgiveness and the like (thus for example the so-called 'preparatory actions' to justification were misunderstood by the Council of Trent). Much as this is the case, faith must be seen fully and fruitfully – that has to be stressed again. It is not the

71

mere assent of understanding and of our will. It has to be the answer of the whole person. Indeed the whole person is accepted by God, and not just his or her understanding or will. And this whole person answers with all that he or she is and does, with thought, feelings and sensibilities, in daily life in all the areas in which it has to be performed and carried out responsibly. In this respect faith and works cannot be separated. Faith is to be a 'faith which is effective in love' (cf. Gal.5.6). Indeed should not faith itself, which is the gateway to new life, to justification, be a *loving* faith and only in this way form the really appropriate answer to God's and Jesus's act of love? Later, now that the heat of the controversies following the Reformation has cooled down, we may be amazed that there could have been such a dispute over it.

The second part of the text from which we began runs:

> For in it the righteousness of God is revealed through faith for faith; as it is written, 'He who through faith is righteous shall live' (Rom.1.17).

It had earlier been said that the gospel is a power of God (Rom.1.16). Now something even more significant is said about it. It contains and reveals the righteousness of God. Here we have the decisive expression the meaning of which we wanted to trace. What does it mean?

Given our terminology, the word righteousness suggests social relationships between persons. Social life should be shaped and ordered righteously, justly; righteous conditions should provide solidarity and security for the individual and a social entity like the community of a village or a city and above all a state. That is a basic presupposition of the existence of people in antiquity stamped with the Graeco-Roman sense of law.

Or we may think of that attitude to righteousness which since the time of Aristotle has been connected with wisdom, boldness and moderation, and regarded as one of the four cardinal virtues. These four are as it were the basic element of true humanity and humane behaviour and are regarded as binding on those who are human. Here righteousness is an attitude which treasures all things in the world, and especially human beings, in accordance with their value, gives them their distinctiveness, and notes their individual rights. A corresponding righteous action should stem from this attitude. Underlying it is a profound sense of reverence which combats any exploitation and manipulation of people and things.

The righteousness which is mentioned in Paul is not, however, of this kind. It has another significance. To understand the expression we must look back into the Old Testament. Righteousness has many meanings there. But one of them predominates, which is completely outlined in terms of Yahweh and thus means *his* righteousness. That is righteousness as a religious and theological concept, which basically denotes what is right, that is, a relationship in accordance with the covenant and made possible by Yahweh between himself and his people (and then also between human beings and their fellows).

However, this relationship is not that of two partners of equal status and with equal rights, but is grounded and established one-sidedly by Yahweh. The covenant is a foundation of Yahweh's grace, it is a covenant of grace. That Yahweh calls his people into this relationship and keeps them in it is a matter of pure gift. The fact that despite all apostasy and lapses he keeps his faith and never revokes the relationship makes this relationship righteous. According to a great many texts righteousness (of God) is another expression for God's goodness, for his grace, his mercy: in short, for his salvation in every way. Of course God can also show his righteousness in judgment and punishment, and this is often threatened, but the positive significance comes out very strongly, frequently in the Psalms and in passages like these:

> But my righteousness will be for ever, and my salvation to all generations (Isa.51.8b)... Thus says the Lord, Keep justice, and righteousness, for soon my salvation will come, and my righteousness be revealed (Isa.56.1).

Paul can take up this view. Without the background of the Old Testament and Jewish literature about the time of Christianity the meaning of the expression would remain obscure, and some errors in interpretation have been caused by this. It is impossible to give detailed references here either to the Old Testament or to that

73

literature, especially the Qumran writings.[24] Recently a good deal of clarity and agreement has been reached over the basic meaning of what Paul is saying.[25]

That the righteousness of God is revealed in the gospel (Rom.1.17) therefore means that God's comprehensive eschatological saving action and his salvation are made known and his saving grace is disclosed to us. Who could arrive at this idea by themselves? Would we not think, if it were a religious and theological and not a philosophical term, that the righteousness which is manifested now represented God's judging and punishing intervention at the end time? We might think that this judgment had been hidden thus far, since God was patiently waiting and being restrained – but now sin has come to make and implement a righteous judgment. What the pious had longingly called for in Israel and the apocalyptists had depicted in bright colours has now come about: righteous judgment on the enemies of God and his people and on all unjust action. Indeed Paul himself could wrongly suggest this view when directly after v.17 he goes on:

> For the wrath of God is revealed from heaven against all ungodliness and wickedness of men who by their wickedness suppress the truth (Rom.1.18).

Would this 'wrath' of God, i.e. his judgment, then be the content of the righteousness of God that I have just depicted? It would be a mistake to think that. The long text which begins with v.18 and runs to 3.20 goes on to give an impressive description of the hopeless state in which pagans and Jews find themselves: hopeless, at any rate, in terms of deliverance in their own strength and without what happened in Jesus Christ. Neither group of people, pagans and Jews, was in a position to find the way to God, although both had splendid possibilities of doing so. Gentiles had access to God through their reason, philosophical knowledge of God and the voice of their conscience (cf. Rom.1.19-21; 2.14f.) and Jews through the excellent gift of the law.

But precisely against this gloomy background, to be painted black on black, in which only a humanity ripe for anger and punishment can be seen, there arises the new liberating message of God's gracious concern which begins abruptly:

> But now the righteousness of God has been manifested apart from law, although the law and the prophets bear witness to it, the righteousness of God through faith in Jesus Christ for all who believe (Rom.3.21,22a).

The 'now' which comes at the beginning marks a deep division and the beginning of changed relationships. It was not the wrath of God which was poured out at this decisive hour but his grace, his righteousness, which no law could produce and which now is aimed only at acceptance in faith. What came was not judgment but great mercy.

Something else must be expressed here which is an essential part of Paul's overall view and has been thought through carefully by him. The gospel discloses the righteousness of God. That applies first of all quite generally and universally, as an offer for everyone; it is even regarded as a cosmic intervention in our world. Sometimes the apostle speaks of his gospel as though it were an independent cosmic entity which comes victoriously into the world bringing salvation, comparable to the powers of disaster (cf. e.g. Phil. 1.27; 2.22; Rom.15.16).

However the righteousness of God must fill the new time not only generally but, as we have already seen come to effect, also in the individual. It is the individual who opens himself or herself to it in faith. It is directed not only globally at humanity as such, as a collective unity which would be blessed by it as a whole. That is at most true in so far as the opportunities which it opens up are open to all without distinction. Rather, it attains its real goal only when it is recognized and grasped by the individual. That happens only in faith, as we saw. When it gets that far, when it is received and accepted, then it recreates people. The old person becomes a new person, one who – wonder of wonders – can stand before God.

This is the process that the apostle means when he speaks of justification. God's righteousness that brings salvation (the righteousness of grace) makes people righteous, and that means those who from now on can live in and from the gracious concern and sanctifying power of God. Moreover, in an important passage in Romans we have both statements linked: God now, i.e. in the end time that is dawning, shows his righteousness and makes righteous the one who believes (Rom.3.26). For the sake of clarity, to resort to jargon once again, we may speak of a 'righteousness-justification'.

Here we must remember two things: first justification always presupposes a verdict on the 'old man', on his inadequacy, his failings, his sin. Only because we are all in the one lost boat and cannot save ourselves from shipwreck is God's involvement 'for us' called on in Paul – otherwise we should all be destroyed. This hopeless and utterly 'sinful' situation is not ignored or concealed, as if God generously wanted to overlook it, just as occasionally we are accustomed to close our eyes or to ignore real wrongdoing. This whole being stands under wrath and judgment (cf. Rom.1.18ff.), and we must also take that seriously, if the standards of good and evil are not to be blurred and arbitrary. But God does not bring about this judgment on us. It is performed vicariously on the one who bore 'our sins', indeed who was himself made sin. As this happened once and for all and applies to all, the way is now free to experience justification as a pardon and as a way to freedom. Or, to put it another way: the judging side of justification, the judgment on the old life, was brought about in the death of Jesus and we have to do only with the side of justification that acquits us. Thus by means of this difficult language and argument we are back again at the heart of Pauline theology, in the message of the death and resurrection of Jesus.

The second thing is that it is quite clear in Paul that God's justifying action extends into the depth of individuals and has a transforming effect. Therefore the word can also be translated 'make righteous', as often happens. God not only declares people righteous but makes them 'holy' through and through.

And those whom he predestined he also called; and those whom he called he also justified; and those whom he justified he also glorified (Rom.8.30).

Here, however, as the apostle understands things, faith and

baptism must be seen together. The faith that justifies receives in baptism the seal that makes it outwardly valid and its consummation. Moreover baptism can only be seen in such a way that it brings about complete justification and sanctification (cf.Rom.6.1-11). The two can be connected, as in this text from I Corinthians: 'But you were washed, you were sanctified, you were justified in the name of the Lord Jesus Christ and in the Spirit of our God' (I Cor.6.11).

Justification by faith and by baptism also follow closely after each other in Galatians:

For in Christ Jesus you are all sons of God, through faith. For as many of you as were baptized into Christ have put on Christ (Gal.3.26f.).

Baptism, too, must always be seen in connection with faith. We cannot pursue all this further, since it would need exhaustive theological comment. I can mention only a few elements, topics in which today Protestant and Catholic interpretation of Paul again coincides and on which it is no longer possible to base divergent church doctrinal traditions, as happened for so long in the past.

Once again in conclusion I should stress what was of decisive importance to the apostle and has remained a pillar in the teaching of the church until today, as it must remain so: this whole work for our blessing, our healing, our deliverance, happened through grace alone. We ourselves could not contribute anything to it or use it; it was for nothing and comes to us as pure gift. No one can ascribe even a scrap of it to himself or herself, and take it to his or her own account. Salvation remains unmerited and unmeritable.

Perhaps we do not have enough understanding of the fact that our forebears at the time of the Reformation could not agree precisely at this point, but went their separate ways. I am not talking about a historical understanding – this has been illuminated for us through scholarship – but about an existential understanding that it could be precisely this question which made the deepest difference.

There may also be the feeling that there are much more important questions in Christianity than that of the conditions for my personal salvation. What is the general destination of humanity? How is the gospel today communicated to those who had no contact with it or got to know it only in diluted form or merely regarded it as the product of a particular culture? Has not the concern for well-being and righteousness and peace for all human beings become far more decisive even for the Christian orientation of life than concern for my own existence before God? We could continue the list of questions further.

Catholics need to understand the Fathers of the Reformation particularly in the way in which they saw the whole of faith preserved or endangered at this point of the *sola gratia* (grace alone), and were essentially right in doing so. If that did not apply without qualification, and if human collaboration were involved in some sense, then one could join in Paul's sharp comments to the Galatians:

> You are severed from Christ, you who would be justified by the law; you have fallen away from grace (Gal.5.4).

Indeed, Christ would have died in vain (cf. Gal.2.11b), the cross of Christ would have been emptied. How could a person somehow want to take part in God's mighty act of deliverance? The thought is absurd. Moreover, to be consistent we would have to maintain a co-involvement in our way of life following baptism, as Paul points out acutely to his opponents in connection with the way of the law. Anyone who still wants to maintain and require that the law (of the Old Testament) and circumcision are necessary for salvation would return again to the level that he or she had just left. He or she would be banished into the existence that we had found to be hopeless:

> Now I, Paul, say to you that if you receive circumcision, Christ will be of no advantage to you. I testify again to every man who receives circumcision that he is bound to keep the whole law (Gal.5.2f.).

What the apostle rejects there decisively, namely the demand from Jews and radical Jewish Christians also to accord a place to obeying the law alongside faith as a factor which brings about salvation, also applies to all other views or practices in which there is some sort of 'collaboration' with salvation in the strict sense. No one can earn heaven, as a once popular phrase put it, nor can God's righteousness be earned through good works, either initially at the beginning of the Christian life or in the future in the divine judgment. Paul has no doubt that in every respect we are to be rich in good works, and he stresses this most emphatically. But the good works are never what one can earn in the understanding I have indicated.

So does this already provide an answer to the questions about the relationship between the achievement of personal salvation and worldwide responsibility for the gospel and for the fate of all human beings which I have mentioned? I do not think so. Rather, it seems that both Protestants and Catholics have often related the Pauline talk of the righteousness of God and the justification of the sinner one-sidedly to the individual situation of a human being, for very different reasons. Luther's question, 'How do I find a gracious God?', is often seen as typical of this and thus as a key to the understanding of Paul's doctrine. But we have seen that the righeousness of God must *a priori* be understood against a universal, eschatological world-embracing horizon. To open oneself to it then also first means to look at the whole of humanity and recognize God's work as a work for all. It would have to be above all a stimulus to reflect on the fact that human beings are to be freed not only from their personal sins and sinful entanglements but also, and indeed first, from a sinful world with its perverted structures. The blatant inequalities, exploitation and humiliation, spiritual and physical terror, wars, hunger and misery – all this and much more that oppresses and shatters us – are almost exclusively sinful conditions caused by human beings. God's mercy and his righteousness are addressed to them, are to be proclaimed in them and to act as stimuli towards overcoming them.

In this sense Pauline doctrine is as much related to Christian service in the world as is the commitment of Jesus to the poor and oppressed. Both are combined in the call to freedom which comes from God and which seeks to make possible a worthwhile life for the individual and for society. Freedom is in truth only one, and it is indivisible. Paul sees it predominantly under the negative perspective of 'freedom from', as liberation from enslaving powers.

But when he tells the Galatians, 'For freedom Christ has set us free' (Gal.5.1,13), he means the whole undivided freedom of the whole person. However, his experience with the crucified Lord shows him even more, namely that someone even in external distress can gain the living power of Christ. We shall be discussing that later (pp.106f.).

8 · The Age of the Spirit

Several times already we have come across the term 'intermediate period', the time between the resurrection of Jesus and the consummation of the world. The decisive development has happened but has not yet been realized to the full. The victory has already been won but it has not yet extended everywhere; the future has already begun but it continues to remain future. In these and similar 'both – and' statements we can attempt to assess the tension which runs through faith and which Paul experienced in himself to breaking point. At one time he speaks as though everything had already been achieved, and then as though everything were still open to the future. In the course of history, too, the weight has shifted at times in thought and sensibility more towards one pole or the other; the present has been experienced as wholly fulfilled and bright or as dark, empty and comfortless. The suffering and terror of the present may move us more strongly today than the hope that is inaugurated, but Paul stresses the presence of salvation which God has created much more strongly than the distress which remains.

But precisely how would he describe this intermediate age? How is the Lordship of Christ confessed by faith realized in it? And how does this new rule work out in the believer and in the group to which he or she belongs, the community or the church? So far these questions have remained open.

We heard much of the negative side when discussing the old world. We are freed from falling victim to this situation, from slavery to its powers. A change of rule took place on a large scale, and takes place on a small scale, where in faith and baptism one is subjected to the new Lord of the new time. This is the starting point, as it were the fact of the new existence.

But Paul found a comprehensive answer for the way in which the Lordship of the Kyrios and life under it are accomplished, an answer which can be given in a word: in the Pneuma, in the Spirit. The Lord exercises his rule in the Spirit. Those under the new rule live their new life in the Spirit, and in his community all that makes them up and belongs to them is achieved and determined by the Spirit. The Pneuma is the nature of the presence of God and the word of God in the intermediate period. Those are the two basic notions, at first presented without explanation. Put as starkly as that they may not seem particularly striking, especially as we are used to hearing and speaking of the Spirit, the Spirit of God or the Holy Spirit.

But what does Paul mean more precisely when he talks of the Spirit, or in Greek of the Pneuma, a term which I often introduce because even the word Spirit has become too pale and nebulous for us in this context. We need to investigate two things: first of all the determination of the Spirit in the life of the individual and then the determination of the Spirit in the community or church (in Paul the same word denotes both: *ekklesia* is the local community and the community = the church everywhere).

Life 'in the Spirit'

Life in the Spirit is a theme which the apostle presents on a broad canvas. Here and there one can pick out a thread and look at it separately. Before we attempt that, though, a general observation must be made: the Pneuma grounds and inspires, supports and accompanies the action of Christians generally; it is the motive force and the principle of the new ethic. According to Paul Christian ethics as a foundation for action and as instruction for it is Pneuma ethics. However, without doubt its foundation is the faith which opens up access to the new life (justification). It is now also the ground and soil from which new action is to grow. The supreme guide is no longer to be fulfilment of the commandment but the fruit of faith. This is a faith which is not lip service, letter, intellectual insight or even a conviction of the understanding or the heart but one which is worked out in action, which brings forth fruits and works, indeed which according to a formula that has become famous and at the same time is a matter of dispute between the confessions, a 'faith working through love':

> For in Christ Jesus neither circumcision nor uncircumcision is of any avail, but faith working through love' (Gal.5.6).

That is faith as the apostle understands it. Certainly everything is given, undeserved and undeservable, including faith. But precisely as a gift of God it is concerned to do abundant and constant good – though doing the good must not come about in a laborious and ultimately fruitless way as service to a law which cannot be fulfilled.

The foundation for action is faith – but the power, the inspiration, the impulse, all come from the Spirit of God. Only in this power of the Spirit can it be possible to bring into being what corresponds to the new basis for life that comes from God. But in this power it should be possible. Both are true. God provides not only this basis for life (righteousness, faith) but also the power to transpose it into concrete action.

In German the word spirit, *Geist*, tends to be associated with understanding, reason, knowledge and the like. If we began from this understanding we would find it difficult to understand Paul and his ethic of the Spirit. In that case we would first always be tempted to think: what I *see* to be good, righteous, helpful and so on should happen. At any rate God's Spirit should help me by guiding my knowledge, by illumination. That would not be wrong; on the contrary. Paul expressly says that the Spirit is the power of the knowledge of faith and its action. God's hitherto hidden secrets are now revealed through the Spirit (cf. I Cor.2.10); the Spirit is communicated to us so that we may know his gifts:

> Now we have received not the spirit of the world, but the Spirit which is from God, that we might understand the gifts bestowed on us by God (I Cor.2.12).

But that is not yet what is meant here.

Paul knows from the Old Testament what spirit is. It is that power through which God creates, brings forth, enlivens, renews.

The Spirit is the power of God, that power which hovered over the waters at the beginning of the world (cf. Gen.1.2) – like a creative potency through which things were to gain life and form from the primal mass. It is also that power through which God will 'renew the face of the earth'. Through God's Spirit the existing state of things is maintained; through it alone can good come into being in us (cf. e.g. Ps.5.12-14). If this power stands behind us, and indeed creates in us, then, Paul says, that to which new life is given must succeed, as must that which it is to produce. However, in our own power we would probably achieve nothing.

This is all the more true for him since he knows far more of God's Spirit than the wise man and suppliant in the Old Testament. That spirit through which our action is to succeed anew is also the Spirit of God's Son himself, the Spirit of Christ; as I Corinthians says: 'But we have the Spirit of Christ' (I Cor.2.16b.). In the Spirit there is an ultimate manifestation, i.e. one going beyond anything that was known previously, of God's primal thought and will, his goodness directed towards us and grasping us. What took place in our favour in the conduct of Jesus, in his commitment, in the surrender even of his life, came from the depths, from the heart of God himself. (I said that it was a matter of love: God's love and Jesus' love are both one for Paul.) So as can be seen there, and as we hear in the hymn in Philippians to the Son who empties himself and is obedient to death, we too should be concerned for one another (cf. Phil.2.5-11); that would be to have 'his mind', the mind of God and the Son, indeed it would already be the Spirit who is meant here. Since we have been accepted, redeemed from the state of slavery and made free sons, we have also received that way of thinking, the spirit of free sons, in which we may enter freely before God – and also behave to one another (even in the church) as free people, without anxiety about new slavery or any kind of new rule: 'And because you are sons, God has sent the Spirit of his Son into our hearts, crying "Abba! Father!"' (Gal.4.5; cf. Rom.8.9: Spirit of Christ). The chapter about the Pneuma in Romans (ch.8) takes this even further; from it we can also see how Paul continues the remarks he begins in the letter to the Galatians:

For you did not receive the spirit of slavery to fall back into fear, but you have received the spirit of sonship. When we cry 'Abba! Father!' it is the Spirit himself bearing witness with our spirit that we are children of God (Rom.8.15f.).

Paul strives higher in order to bring out the new starting situation; to our minds almost excessively high. Or does this seem to us so high only because our experience knows too little of the life in the Spirit since in our ethical action we calculate, weigh, reflect, orientate ourselves on the milieu and on customs to a much greater degree, rather than leave ourselves to the impulse that seeks to work in us?

Certainly the apostle means to be taken at his word when he says that we have 'received' the Spirit; that it is 'given' to us (Gal.3.2,5; cf. II Cor.11.3), indeed that it lives in us as in a house (I Cor.3.16; Rom.8.9), and that it really is the Spirit of God himself and not just a contact with him, a shadow, a breath of him.

The realism of such expressions arises from the fact that Paul not only affirms the transformation from the 'old' to a 'new' man in general terms and in his faith but that the change is experienced in a very specific process accessible to the senses, namely in baptism. There what faith acknowleges as 'justification', 'making righteous', 'sanctification', 'acceptance as son' is made known and also represented in an event which can be experienced outwardly. Baptism is receiving the Spirit, the gift to the new person who is raised out of the water to new life of the dowry of the Spirit. Paul calls this dowry a firstfruit (thus in Rom.8.23) or a pledge in the sense of a down-payment (thus in II Cor.1.22; 5.5). That means that it is not yet the total, the full sum – but it is a real beginning of it. It is not to be thought of as a ticket which must be given in when the performance begins, or as a pawn ticket which is only good for the surrender of the object it represents. Both these would be only tokens of the object itself, not even a bare substitute for it or even a part in it, but credentials for a later participation or for the return of the pledge.

Paul uses a matter-of-fact expression from commerce (down payment = deposit), but he does not see God as a trading partner.

Yet this language is meant to be taken realistically as denoting a share in the substance itself: the substance itself is the whole, salvation, consummation, the kingdom of God. Now, already, God gives that 'firstfruit' of it which comes from the whole harvest, the 'down-payment' which is already deducted from the whole sum.

So we could also say that we already have that salvation in its overflowing fullness, in the manner of the Pneuma, the Spirit of God. What is already given of the whole has been given in the manner of the Spirit as Spirit, pneumatically. The Pneuma is the kind of presence of the whole of salvation which was disclosed in Jesus Christ, which fills the intermediate period. It does not mean that you already have a share of the Spirit, as though it were also the whole gift in the future. It means that what you have received now is part of the whole, and you have received it as the Spirit of God's Son.

And indeed in that case the basis for this realism is that we too may hope by virtue of this spirit of the resurrection, an event which for the apostle is as real as it is in the case of Jesus himself. As our fate is inseparably fused with his (cf. Rom.6.3-11), this prospect of the end is certain for us; as the triumphant statement in Romans has it:

> If the Spirit of him who raised Jesus from the dead dwells in you, he who raised Christ Jesus from the dead will give life to your mortal bodies also through his Spirit which dwells in you (Rom.8.11; cf. also I Cor.15.22).

One could contrast the two in a somewhat schematic way. Earlier the message for the Jews (and also for the Gentiles) who were bound to a principle of the law and could only seek their opportunities there was: 'You shall.' But now for the one who allows himself to be accepted by God in the Son the message is: 'You may and you can. There is a power for good in you which certainly needs your assent and your cooperation, but it now will no longer give rise to the feeling that you are left to yourself and your own strength. Whatever good comes out of you is the "*fruit* of the Spirit"', attractively presented by Paul in opposition to the '*works* of the flesh' (the *sarx*). The fruits of the Spirit are 'love, joy, peace,

patience, kindness, goodness, faithfulness, gentleness, self-control'
(Gal.5.19, 22; cf. Rom.14.17). That power for good which is and
is called the Spirit of God will be at work in such fruits.

Paradoxically enough, Paul can describe the new situation of
people who believe as service, the very word used of slavery. It is
the same word but it relates to different basic situations. This
service now arises out of the free obedience of children to a father,
and no longer from subjection by contemptuous slave owners.

But now we are discharged from the law, dead to that which held
us captive, so that we serve not under the old written code but
in the new life of the Spirit (Rom.7.6).

Slavery was servitude to the letter – because it was serving the
law – but now service can be done in the freedom of the Spirit.

Who has qualified us to be ministers of a new covenant, not in a
written code but in the Spirit; for the written code kills, but the
Spirit gives life (II Cor.3.6).

Nevertheless the apostle also sees the situation in a matter-of-
fact way, experiences the dangers and sees deep divisions, as in
Corinth; and also knows above all from his own experience the
infinite troubles and struggles in which the new life must also be
asserted tenaciously and with a good grace. He sees backsliding,
timorous thinking, arrogance, egoism and so on in the communities.
Nevertheless he does not make any cuts in his total remarks about
the new life and the Spirit nor will he tone down the claim that such
a life makes in itself and to which it is directed. I think that he
cannot and may not do this because this ethic was not outlined by
him, indeed was not thought up and formulated by human beings
at all, but is grounded in God's own action. Who could dare to take
away, diminish, weaken anything in what God himself has devised
and put to work and thus want to tailor it to a much more
comfortable human standard? Paul would probably have regarded
this as an intervention in God's own work, and an intervention in
what for him represents justification by faith and grace alone. At
one point he says this quite clearly:

For God has not called us for uncleanness but in holiness. Therefore whoever disregards this disregards not man but God, who gives his Holy Spirit to you (I Thess. 4.7f.)

However, there must also be firm contours, a clear content, commandments and prohibitions in such a Pneuma ethic. 'Spirit ethic' does not mean that everything is made optional and can be left vague, that only the particular situation and a particular mood that we feel are normative. Paul openly says that the commandments of God are to be kept (I Cor.7.19); he therefore knows that the whole law is fulfilled in the commandment to love (cf. Rom.13.8-10), indeed he can even speak of the new ethos as the law of Christ (Gal.6.2), as if using a formula. But this all now applies on the new basis, in the power of God given for fulfilment; it holds in the power of the impulse of the Pneuma:

But if you are led by the Spirit you are not under the law (Gal.5.18).

But there are also contrary forces which tend towards corruption and so lead people astray into every form of wickedness. Paul is also quite clear about the negative side of ethical decisions and modes of behaviour; he often mentions wrong forms of behaviour and prohibits them. Even here everything has by no means become 'voluntary', say on the basis of a higher consciousness, as though now that people have the Spirit they are raised above, indeed taken out of, all primitive decisions over good and evil and all conventions in this sphere, so that new generous criteria apply there and no danger is to be feared from pettiness – a situation rather like that endorsed by popular moral ideas, according to which the 'great' in the world are also allowed more generous criteria, whereas the lesser are given no concessions but everything is required of them punctiliously. The apostle knows nothing of such liberality, which also occurred frequently in history. The works of the flesh (the *sarx*), i.e. of the human being who egoistically focusses on himself and selfishly seeks his own advantage, can be seen clearly:

Now the works of the flesh are plain: immorality, impurity, licentiousness, idolatry, sorcery, enmity, strife, jealousy, anger, selfishness, dissension, party spirit, envy, drunkenness, carousing and the like. I warn you, as I warned you before, that those who do such things shall not inherit the kingdom of God (Gal.5.19-21).

'Sarx' literally means flesh. When Paul uses it in contrast to spirit he means the 'natural' man in his thinking and efforts related to himself; moreover one can also translate the word in a somewhat narrow way as 'self-seeking'. In an irreconcilable and uncompromising opposition of spirit and flesh, pneuma and sarx, a life according to the pneuma or according to the sarx, the apostle gives an effective description of the past and the newly given overall direction of life, especially in Galatians and Romans (cf. the passages in Gal.5.13-26 and in Rom.8.1-17; the latter is not easy to understand).

Life in the Spirit is, as I said, a wide-ranging and major theme in Paul. We get the strongest impression of it if we read Romans 8 carefully. There are flashes and glints on all sides, a whole series of visions and prospects.

Life in the Spirit means two things. On the one hand it is given (with initial grace, justification, baptism and so on, cf. I Cor.6.11b); on the other hand it is lived out. There too there is the tension between an 'already' and a 'not yet' which we came upon once before. Where, as here, the tension relates to action, to specific doing, it is described as tension between indicative and imperative, between present possession and future proving of what has been given, between gift and task, is and ought, or with other similar phrases. It is precisely the magnitude of the gift which is to be matched by a similarly great, unselfish action, ultimately formed by love and directed towards it. Paul has coined a classical phrase for this that is virtually impossible to translate: 'If we live in the pneuma/spirit, then let us also walk in the pneuma/spirit' (Gal.5.25).

That means something like this: we exist from this new reality, from the spirit-power of God, that disposition of God which was communicated to us. Now we should and indeed will also shape our life in praxis in accordance with this reality and to match it.

This is as it were the principle which has now to be followed: to live in accordance with the Spirit because our actions are fundamentally impelled by the Spirit. God himself creates good actions through us by his good Spirit. This brief sentence is a summary of the new ethos to which God calls and invites us, and for which he equips those who accept this call: 'If we live in the Spirit, then let us also walk in the Spirit.'

This sentence contains everything that the apostle works out in detail – almost inexhaustibly – and to which he summons people, by admonitions, by gracious fatherly or sharp comradely advice, by promise and encouragement, by recollection of what his hearers have been told earlier and a development of it, by invitation and request. We find all this in his letters to churches – and it all comes from the same Spirit in which he himself thinks and speaks (cf. I Cor.7.40) and in which Christians are also to speak and act.

'For freedom Christ has set us free' (Gal.5.1) – that sounds like a watchword, a splendid slogan which arouses a deep echo in us. Is it not also a seductive slogan which could wrongly suggest a complete lack of ties and indeed arbitrariness? The words of the apostle were in fact understood in this way by those people who followed only individual sayings and did not listen to all that Paul conveys. He himself sees the danger clearly and identifies it: the danger that the new freedom could itself lead to new slavery, slavery to the self, self-seeking (the flesh), whereas it should in truth be liberation for one another and towards one another:

For you were called to freedom, brethren; only do not use your freedom as an opportunity for the flesh, but through love be servants of one another (Gal.5.13; cf. also Rom.5.5).

And when there is any question of mutual admonition and instruction, this should happen in the Spirit, which here is described as the spirit of gentleness:

If a man is overtaken in any trespass, you who are spiritual should restore him in the spirit of gentleness. Look to yourself, lest you too be tempted (Gal.6.1).

But Paul prefers to keep to the general statements which recall the foundation of the new life created by God as that to which he constantly refers in his many individual admonitions, as in this example. However, both factors are always present in his writings: God's initiative and work and our own concern to grasp it and do it with our own will. So he can say, without actually mentioning the Spirit:

Therefore my beloved... work out your own salvation in fear and trembling; for God is at work in you, both to will and to work for his good pleasure (Phil.2.12f.).

At this point I would like to pause for a moment. The question arises how what the apostle has experienced and grasped deeply is related to what determines and supports our own action. Of course that cannot be expounded here in full, but I would like to mention one point. Is the orientation for our action which seeks to be 'Christian' and certainly often enough actually is – at least in intent and direction – determined underneath by a mere 'should', and indeed by a 'law' and obedience towards it? Is Christianity nevertheless a kind of religion of the law? The view often seems to be firmly rooted in a particular Catholic feeling that Christian life is concerned with 'fulfilling the commandments'. For example, for generations the questions to be asked in self-examination were based on the Ten Commandments, and all the ramifications and specialized questions which sought to focus more sharply on the present situation remained indebted to this model.

Over the past few decades there has certainly been a stronger concentration on the central demand of love – but even this could still be understood in the traditional understanding as a commandment – and only in that way. Certainly here it becomes much more strikingly obvious and clear to the individual how great the distance is between task and actual fulfilment, and how wide the gap indeed often is between the two. Many will have resorted to common sayings like, 'I do the best I can' – 'God takes good intentions into account' (and that should be enough) – 'I'm only human and have my limitations' – or even 'I am a sinner before him and always will be'.

The question which presses in on me is whether we have really

91

accepted and tried out the Pauline conviction of having God's Spirit as a power for achievement. Paul also knows that Christians can fulfil commandments, above all, of course, the demand of love, as we saw. And his idea of a 'Christian life' is no less or no narrower than it was in the call of Jesus to the disciples and the criteria which he gives for that (cf. the Sermon on the Mount, Matt.5-7). But Paul knows that secret power in us which compels and urges us on to fulfilment. Christian ethics as ethics of the Spirit seems to me still – or again – to be a land waiting to be discovered. Perhaps that is connected with the fact that we have largely forgotten or lost this dimension, or indeed both, with the result that we demonstrate so much mediocrity, contentment with what seems achievable, familiarity with compromise, and often prove to be so unattractive. I don't know, but I think that there may well be a connection here.

9 · 'In the Spirit' – 'in Christ'

So far we have spoken of the Pneuma almost as if it were connected with the individual and his or her personal life, as if it were that power which is bestowed on each one for his or her own career. But Paul always addresses *all* those to whom his letters are sent; even in the small private letter to Philemon. For him they *a priori* belong together as a unity. As we are accustomed to say, they are a community (*ekklesia*). We must now turn to this reality. Our attention is again directed to the new situation after Christ. The move in thought to which we are invited is not a difficult one. I would put it like this: in Jesus Christ God has radically changed the situation of the world, transformed a hopeless situation into a new one, destined to life and again endowed with hope. Just as the old world had its symbol in the old Adam, so the new world received one in Christ. Of course this was and is more than a symbol, more than as it were a purely negative or positive sign. For just as death was really present at the end as the only prospect, so now life is really there. But the new situation should be recognized by people, accepted; the hope should be grasped – everything has indeed happened for our sakes – and at what a price and commitment! But where people take up this word of hope and make it their word, begin to live from it, there God's action achieves its first aim; it does not remain empty or as it were suspended in mid-air, like a lamp in a lighthouse or a slogan which a plane writes on the sky: 'It's the new time!' Where people follow the call and allow it to mark a decisive beginning (in faith and baptism), they enter a community which is already founded in God.

What sort of a community is that? Evidently it is not formed in the same way as other committees and associations, with collaboration and agreements, the formulation of aims, the drawing up of rules, the establishment of conditions and so on. Here things are quite different because the community comes from somewhere completely different and is given to us. We spoke of the death of Jesus, which is inwardly permeated with 'for you', 'for us'. Jesus's death itself already included in the will and obedience of that 'for', the fact that it was to be a death for us all. So we may also say that the death of Jesus was already on behalf of a community which would recognize it as its deliverance and take it to itself. There Paul seems to see the roots of what then also appeared openly and as a social entity as 'community'. However, that could only happen when God had confirmed this 'for' in favour of human beings in the resurrection of Jesus, with his 'yes'.

The 'for us' of Jesus' death and God's 'yes' to it (cf. II Cor.1.19f.) apply without qualification to all, so that no individual may be excluded. But both the 'for us' and the 'yes' have an effect only where they are proclaimed and believed. This proclamation and belief bring into being in visible and tangible form the community for which Jesus lived and died and in which the Risen One now lives. Moreover, this has brought about more than an outward gathering on the basis of the same destiny and the same experience of the word of proclamation, comparable with other shared destinies which may come into being among the survivors of a catastrophe, comrades in war who have come through a situation which seemed to be hopeless,or among members of a heroic expedition. Believers find a pre-existing 'spiritual' community which had been hidden in God's plan and which was then founded on the death and resurrection of Jesus.

Although the 'community' then appears as a social formation which thinks, acts, celebrates and generally lives together, it remains inwardly what it is from the beginning: a spiritual community, a community 'in the Spirit', a people under the rule of its Lord, the work of God. In the thought of the apostle the community or church is not the sum of many individuals but a totality 'in the Lord'. All together form a kind of sphere of rule in which he is regarded as, and called on as, the Kyrios.

And not only do individuals receive the Spirit when they become

Christians, but they are all one body, one Pneuma-reality; they live as community 'in the Spirit'. Paul expresses clearly what we can only understand and describe with difficulty. We found a similar difficulty when we were trying to understand Paul's view of the powers of disaster and their universal rule. Here we are concerned with the positive realities which Paul also sees as such manifestations transcending the individual. There is a common 'being in the Lord', a 'being in the Spirit'; there is community and church as the 'body of Christ'. In Romans we find, 'But you are not in the flesh, you are in the Spirit, if the Spirit of God really dwells in you. Anyone who does not have the Spirit of Christ does not belong to him' (Rom.8.9). And even more comprehensibly in I Corinthians: 'For by one Spirit we were all baptized into one body – Jews or Greeks, slave or free – and all were made to drink of one Spirit' (I Cor.12.13). We can probably say with some justification that the three forms of expression, 'In the Spirit/Pneuma', 'in Christ' and being 'one body in Christ' constantly refer to the same reality, each under its own aspect.

Paul's characteristic terminology is 'being in Christ'. We do not need much help towards understanding this strange and much-discussed expression given all that has been said so far. However, the special aspect which is introduced above all with the name Christ – as opposed to 'being in the Pneuma' must be given particular emphasis. Talk of an existence in the Spirit, of a life determined by the Pneuma, could also have dangerous connotations, as we have already seen. Even if it may seem remarkable and indeed alien to our usual thought and ideas for people to have believed that they had been set free in the Spirit of God from everyday conditions and were hovering in a higher world – there were those who did in fact think in this way. Paul met them in Corinth and recognized them as a deadly danger.

Life in the Spirit does not transpose us into higher spheres, does not take us out of laborious daily tribulations, does not leave us in existence in the body – perhaps distressing existence – while our real self, which finds it painful to endure its earthly remains, has soared far above and settled in the beyond (perhaps this is a way of thinking carried on underground down the centuries, and not all that exceptional and alien: some idealistic views, as in Karl May and, say, anthroposophy may be fed from this stream from antiquity). Paul as it were ties the Spirit of God to the heavy, earthly person of Jesus Christ. The Spirit with which we have to do, or better, which has to do with us, is the Spirit of Jesus Christ, the Spirit of the one who was man as we are (cf.Rom.8.3) and who now lives in the glory of the Father. He was a true and real person, not an airy spiritual being after the fashion of the 'powers of this world', of which Paul can also speak (cf. I Cor.2.6,8; according to the views of antiquity they inhabited and dominated the universe), or an angel, an angelic being. No, he was a human being whose humanity was demonstrated unsurpassably for the apostle in his utterly human and fearful death and who was then freed from this death into new life in God. Paul speaks of him principally as the Son of God and as the Lord (so we also find the formula 'in the Lord' very frequently) and as Jesus Christ or also just Jesus or Christ. This last terminology constantly denotes the one who was killed and risen. There is no exception to this strict rule. If we see this, we can perhaps understand better why it is of decisive importance for Paul to see that the Spirit is the Spirit of (Jesus) Christ (Rom.8.9); indeed he can even say conversely that the Lord himself is the Spirit (II Cor.3.17). Being in Christ means being a new creation (II Cor.5.17) and thus being taken up into the mode of existence which God has created in him and made possible for all of us. There are many facets of this typical Pauline terminology, and the apostle has many different ways of using it; it is one of his favourite phrases. What underlies it?

When speaking of the Pneuma as a comprehensive reality, in other words not just as a gift given to the individual, I resorted to the use of the somewhat colourless expression 'sphere' ('sphere of lordship'). We must also apply it here. Where Christ has become in believers, in the community, the one who now determines, directs, illuminates, strengthens, moulds in his good Spirit the whole of life, there comes into being a 'sphere' of his presence in which he lives.

Does the experience of being in love and of real love among human beings give us some kind of parallel to this thought? For the lover the world looks different and new, and in one sense is it not indeed different and new? Everything that happens to him or her is bathed in light and in a feeling of happiness. Everything seems to be changed, outside and in. The beloved is indeed really present, and the lover tries to see with his or her eyes, to think with his or her thoughts, indeed to become one with him or her. This is a spiritual presence, certainly, but is it not real? And if many people 'adore' someone, not enthusiastically or after the fashion of the cult of pop stars, but because they are touched by the mystery and emanation of their person, does that not produce a common bond, a spiritual association in the one who is adored? These may be only small steps towards understanding, but perhaps they do take us some way towards what for Paul is the meaning of the name and the person of Jesus Christ. He can say that the whole community is 'in him', as in the addresses in the letters, like that to the community in Thessalonica, which is 'in God the Father and in the Lord Jesus Christ' (I Thess.1.1), or to that of Corinth whose members are addressed as 'the saints in Christ Jesus' (I Cor.1.2; cf. Phil.4.21; I Thess.2.14). It can be said of collaborators or particularly prominent members of the community that they are fellow-workers in Christ (cf. Rom.16.9,10; Philemon 23). Sometimes one can even understand the expression as a way of saying 'being a Christian' or 'Christian'; someone who is in Christ is a Christian (cf. I Cor.3.1; 4.10,15,17). But we only perceive the authentic Pauline echo when there is a completely personal relationship in the expression in which the nearness of this person Jesus Christ is experienced. That means more than a sphere of lordship and salvation in which Christ is present. Paul means to say that he himself belongs to Christ and lives in his refreshing and consoling presence, indeed – in a very dense saying – he says that he himself is in us. Romans 8 begins with a statement which is to be taken to be a general comment on Christian existence: 'There is therefore no condemnation for those who are in Christ Jesus' (Rom.8.1).

But a couple of sentences later Paul can say in a concentrated form,

But if Christ is in you, although your bodies are dead because of sin, your spirits are alive because of righteousness' (Rom.8.10).

As we saw, in essence that amounts to what is being said in the surrounding remarks about the Spirit of God and the Spirit of Christ, but we can also see a distinctive nuance in it: he himself is in us, he whose life we know and on whose thought we are orientated (cf. Phil.2.5). Such well known and bold sayings as 'I live no longer, but Christ lives in me' (Gal.2.20) indicate that we are on the right track here. Christ is the one who loved Paul and gave himself for him, as the passage goes on to say. Here is someone in whom Paul may believe (Gal.2.20b).

Christ in us, we in him – that is like a puzzle picture. We must try to think it out. We shall understand something of what Paul means and says from his experience only if we have in mind that love of Christ which he experienced and praised. It makes him greet the Corinthian community with these words: 'My love is with you all in Christ Jesus' (I Cor.16.24). That may be the key to such insights.

10 · The Body of Christ

I said that the many who belong to one body, one community, are a new entity, not just the sum of many parts. This unity is already outlined for them in advance, as it were prepared, in God's thought and has a real foundation in the death of Jesus. Paul feels the unity from God so strongly that he dares to say that the many who are so different in origin (Jew-Greek), social status (slave-free) and sex (male-female) have become one in Christ Jesus. The differences among them which sometimes open up great gaps (slave-free) no longer play a role, indeed *now* they are no longer considerable. Nor do they denote different starting points and opportunities for being able to fulfil one's life (as between Gentile and Jew), so that the one would *a priori* be in a more favourable situation than the other. Before God and specifically 'in' Christ they are all equal when they have been baptized and put on Christ (like a new garment),[26] indeed they have all together become one, one person. Listen to this amazing text:

> For as many of you as were baptized into Christ have put on Christ. There is neither Jew nor Greek, there is neither slave nor free, there is neither male nor female, for you are all one in Christ Jesus (Gal.3.27f.).

Paul did not draw the social consequences of such a view of the community, above all in respect of ancient slavery and the high estimation of man as over against woman which was familiar to him through Judaism.[27] He probably thought through and fought against the consequences of the abolition of the division between Jews and 'Greeks' (or Gentiles) because in this case it was a matter of the way in, the opportunity for salvation. And he had to fight unyieldingly over it: 'the righteousness of God' comes from 'grace and faith alone', 'apart from the law' (cf. Rom.3.21).[28] Why may he not have acted in this way in the two other cases (slave-free, male-female)? There can be no doubt about this: he did not see it as his task to proclaim a basic alteration in social conditions and abuses, because he felt that time was in any case too short, because he wanted to use the span of his proclamation of the gospel (cf. Rom.15.18-29) up to the glorious coming of Christ (his *parousia*) fully for this work which he knew to be his most basic commission (cf. Gal.1.15f.). So he also gave instructions for each person to remain in the status in which he or she was called (to faith) – instructions which the apostle makes in an authoritarian way that becomes understandable to us only on the basis of his sense of urgency, with only a brief interval left. The context from which I have quoted contains the statement, 'the appointed time has grown very short' (I Cor.7.29). If the next text sounds strange to us, we should not overlook the fact that the basic insight of Galatians, that they are all one in Christ, is nevertheless implied (in the case of slaves it is very clear):

> Only, let every one lead the life which the Lord has assigned to him, and in which God has called him. This is my rule in all the churches. Was any one at the time of his call already circumcised? Let him not seek to remove the marks of circumcision. Was any one at the time of his call uncircumcised? Let him not seek circumcision. For neither circumcision counts for anything nor uncircumcision, but keeping the commandments of God. Every one should remain in the state in which he was called. Were you a slave when called? Never mind. But if you can gain your freedom, avail yourself of the opportunity. For he who was called in the Lord as a slave is a freedman of the Lord. Likewise he who was free when called is a slave of Christ. You were bought with a price; do not become slaves of men. So brethren, in whatever state each was called, there let him remain with God (I Cor.7.17-24).

In our view this would be an interim rule for the time that has grown short, as is evident from I Cor.7.29. But in that case it must

100

not be regarded as an apostolic instruction which should be handed down as such literally without reference to the social requirements, above all when it comes to the position of women in the community and then in society. Our church fathers should have continued to build on the foundation laid in Gal.3.28 before these urgent questions began to force themselves on the church as they do today, first from outside the church.

From the idea that all those who are baptized are 'one in Christ' it is only a short step to the remark that they are one body, that the community or church is the body of Christ. That again has a familiar echo for Catholic sensibilities. Not only is this view deeply connected with a new experience among the generation after the First World War – above all in Germany; it also had a considerable effect for a long time as a result of an encyclical by Pope Pius XII with the title and theme 'On the mystical body of Christ' (*Mystici corporis Christi*, 1943). To be able to see the church not only as a body and organization with an external constitution, hierarchical structure and strict divisions in terms of status and authority, but as a mystery inwardly grounded in Christ, gave many people a new dimension in their awareness of the church. Moreover this view continued to be stressed strongly right down to the Second Vatican Council, its most impressive and dominant perspective being that of the church as the people of God.

However, something must now be said about this favourite Catholic child – in the light of Paul – which many people may find sobering. This is in no way a central idea or a dominant view for him. The expression comes up quite incidentally. If we look more closely, we also find differences. The apostle uses the picture of the body once as a *comparison* with the interconnection of the various tasks and gifts (the 'gifts of grace') in the community. That was not a completely original thought – on the contrary.

This comparison appears often in Greek and Roman literature, particularly in Stoic philosophy, which Paul also knew. There indeed it plays a considerable role as a theoretical model for life in an ordered world. Just as the various members of the body have different functions, each individual for himself or herself, but are also all needed together if the organism is to remain healthy, so too the same thing should happen in social contexts: in a family, in the city and above all in the state. In order to produce a harmonious order, not only is each individual made aware of having an indispensable place in the whole and of fulfilling his own particular task, but this picture of social order is also aimed at achieving accord with the order and harmony of the world. The organism of the world which stands in a meaningful and large-scale interplay with all cosmic forces is to be the model which is to be reflected in social and political institutions on earth. That is the way in which the Stoics see it.

Paul finds this image and the use of the *comparison* for social relationships ('like the members in a body') already in existence. He takes it up and applies it to the community. The ideas are familiar to us and there is a long explanation of them in I Corinthians, partly with almost curious caricatures of the image (I Cor.12.14-16). He is concerned with the unity of the community and harmony in it. 'As it is, there are many parts, yet one body' (I Cor.12.20). Individuals are to understand themselves only as members and to serve the building up and health of the whole body. Each person is not there for himself or herself, but all are there for the whole. In that case it also makes for peaceable participation in the life and task of the other if all are aware of the whole:

If one member suffers, all suffer together; if one member is honoured, all rejoice together (I Cor.12.26).

With this illuminating comparison the apostle seeks to arouse mutual understanding, to damp down an egotistic overvaluation of a gift ('glossolalia'[29]), to help others with outwardly less striking functions, and to stress their importance too. The comparison is thus used for a practical purpose to make evident and support the admonition to peacefulness. The character of the comparison is quite clear and illuminating even today: *just as* the many members must exercise their own activities for the well being of the whole body, *so* too it must be among you today. Body and community will only be able to thrive if each member plays its part for the benefit of the whole. So far there are no difficulties in understanding.

That only begins where the language ceases to become that of a simile, where there is talk of a real body and the community/church is itself called body. There the language of simile is left behind and the terminology goes on to another plane. However, that happens only three times in all the letters. Nevertheless this image was a natural one for Paul to use of the church, as we saw. He did not, however, develop it further so that it became an ecclesiology (doctrine of the church) – at least not in the texts of his which we have. This happens only in Colossians and Ephesians, in which the shoots in Paul have grown into stately trees. Above all in Ephesians, we have a doctrine of the church as the body of Christ. Christ is the head (an idea which Paul does not express), and we all are members of this body (cf. Col.1.18,24; 2.19; 3.15; Eph.1.22f.; 2.6; 4.12, etc.).

Paul himself is sparing, but his hints are illuminating. A passage in Romans comes nearest to the idea of unity in Christ which we found in Gal. 3.28 ('you are "one" in Christ'). There the image of the body as a comparison, as we found it in I Corinthians, is introduced and carried through in terms of the context, with the addition that they are 'one body in Christ'. In the community they are not only to behave as members in a body but they are in fact such a body, in that new reality for which Paul uses the term 'being in Christ'.

For as in one body we have many members, and all the members do not have the same function, so we, though many, are one body in Christ, and individually members one of another (Rom.12.4f.).

Of the individual it can be said that he is 'in Christ'; it can also be said – though only at this point – that the community exists similarly as a whole as a 'body' 'in Christ' (cf. I Cor.12.27).

The third passage is even more illuminating because it indicates how Paul may have thought of this being a body in more detail. The starting point here is the experience of the Lord's Supper, as he calls this central activity of the community (I Cor.11.20; cf.10.21). The bread is distributed with the saying that it is the 'body of Christ' – as the apostle has it from the tradition into which he enters and which he takes over (cf. I Cor.1.23). The many assembled there eat of the same bread, which is his body, the body given in death and for us. Would it not be natural to extend this idea about the community rather further? Say in this direction: the bread that is distributed, which is the body of Christ, brings about communion among all – all eat of the same food. It is one and the same bread which all receive and which feeds them all – so as table companions and as participants in the same food they belong closely together through this food. Those who eat of the gift which is his body as it were become one body. If we leave out this 'as it were', then we have the idea which dawns on Paul. It may not seem so extraordinary to us, since we are accustomed to listening to it and thinking about it. But when it happened for the first time it was surely different. The bread/a body – the community/a body and both combined in the same expression, body of Christ. As a whole the text runs:

> The cup of blessing which we bless, is it not a participation in the blood of Christ? The bread which we break, is it not a participation in the body of Christ? Because there is one loaf, we who are many are one body, for we all partake of the same loaf (I Cor.10.16f.).

We may surely go yet one stage further in our interpretation and take up an idea which has become very important to me and which I have found to be liberating. If the body is formed through the bread which is given as 'body of Christ' and as this body points to the one who was given over to death, then the community should also be understood in terms of this movement of love, of surrender, when the eucharist is celebrated. That would not happen in order to celebrate the community and church as the body of Christ and to praise the glory with which it is endowed in him – which would correspond more with the view in Colossians and Ephesians – but for it to be taken up into the movement of devout service for others: eucharist not as the conclusion of a memorial service for others, but as a disclosure for them. That could come very close to a missionary openness of the eucharist, a dimension which has often been felt necessary and has been looked for, but has often enough been brought up only at the time of the old closing greeting, *ita missa est*, in the somewhat pompous sense of, 'Off you go, now it's time for mission'. In accordance with Pauline thinking we may say that the community receives the body of Christ which has been given so that it may itself be and become a body, a body which similarly seeks to live from the law of the 'for you', which seeks to become what was so often asserted at Vatican II, a serving church.

11 · Jesus' Life and Death in Us

If we want to go on reflecting on this last point, we must bring in the key term 'intermediate period'. We know that its main feature was the new reality of the Pneuma, the Spirit. The intermediate period between the resurrection of Jesus and his parousia is the time of the Pneuma. And as we heard, the Pneuma is the Pneuma, the Spirit, of Jesus Christ. When Paul uses the name Jesus or Christ or combines the two as 'Jesus Christ' he always means the one who is dead *and* risen. We have also discussed that. In that case might one conclude that the intermediary period, the time of the Pneuma, is stamped by the one who died and rose again, that it contains in it both sides of the Christ event? If we want to follow Paul we may and indeed must think in those terms. In the Pneuma Christ remains present in time; he and his fate are not to be regarded as an individual event lying in past history. The Lordship of Christ, his being Kyrios, is exercised and made present in and as Pneuma. The present mode of Lordship is hidden, withdrawn into the world of God, only to be accepted, to be believed, to be acknowledged in the Spirit: 'No one can say Jesus is Lord except by the Holy Spirit' (I Cor.12.3b).

Now the decisive thing is that not only does the Risen One with his powers and his glory remain present in this time and determine its character but his activity also extends to the dead. Christ is the one who combines and represents both in himself. We have to do with both realities, the new world supported by hope, living in the powers of God, grasped in faith – but also with the fallen, sullied, hostile old world which is extremely difficult to rob of its powers. Paul stresses the presence of the new most strongly; this also indisputably remains the first and most important thing. But he

106

also experiences opposing powers, the failures which introduce corruption, opposition, pressure towards death. Both factors together stamp the existence of the believer. Indeed it sometimes seems as if the believer is caught up in this conflict and torn apart by it. But in his own person and with his exposed life Paul is an indication that one need not be torn apart and destroyed in this conflict. Here perhaps we touch on the nucleus of his existence as a Christian and as an apostle. We could hardly dare to say anything about that had he himself not done so. Let us listen to a text from II Corinthians:

> We are afflicted in every way, but not crushed; perplexed, but not driven to despair; persecuted, but not forsaken; struck down, but not destroyed (II Cor.4.8f.; cf. also I Cor.4.10-13).

Each time all seems at an end and lost, but ultimately a chance of survival always appears. Now in itself such an antithetical series as we have here would not be completely singular, utterly unique. It could also describe a chain of happy circumstances, unusual pieces of good fortune, indeed be an optimistic expression of a bold 'not letting oneself be got down' and the like. But this is precisely what the apostle does not want to say. Rather, he wants to bear witness that the power to withstand and survive does not come from him but from God. As he puts it elsewhere, 'I can do all things in him who strengthens me' (Phil.4.13).

The glorious gospel is entrusted to him, but it is a treasure in earthen vessels. His overburdened and threatened life is a fragile vessel for such a supreme content, for such a treasure. It is only thanks to the strength of God that the vessel is not yet broken; this is the same experience with God which we have already come across when Paul was speaking of his deep distress in mortal danger (cf.II Cor.1.8-11):

> But we have this treasure in earthen vessels, to show that the transcendent power belongs to God and not to us (II Cor.4.7).

This sentence comes before the list of distresses that I quoted earlier. But at this point we are taken one stage further. Not only has God's power proved itself in his weakness, the power of the one 'who raises the dead' (cf. II Cor.1.9); there is something further and more mysterious to say. The suffering which he has to bear is *the suffering of Jesus* (cf. II Cor.1.5); the death which constantly reaches out for him is the death which overcame Jesus. Since Damascus he has become the servant of Christ, has entered into communion with him, is so caught up in his fate that suffering has become Christ's suffering for him (cf.also Phil.3.10). Or to put it another way: he senses that he still belongs to the old age which has been given its valid symbol in the cross of Christ, although he knows and says, 'The world is crucified to me and I to the world' (Gal.6.14).

But because the 'old world' still storms powerfully around him and over him, the apostle of the victorous gospel, and indeed tries to muzzle him and destroy him, he can understand these tribulations, too, only in the sign of the cross, in fellowship with the dead Jesus. He recognizes in them that he really belongs to Christ; indeed they are the credentials for his association with him: the Lord is *also*, as I said, present to our time as the one who died. Indeed we may go further and at least suppose that *if* the apostle were to serve without these assaults, without suffering, but as a victorious hero and a celebrated star, he might doubt whether he belonged to Christ, indeed might ask whether he had not failed in his calling. Precisely for this reason he also dares to show his suffering in his work as an apostle as proof of his authentic and true apostleship – in the long catalogue of suffering of which I spoke at the beginning (II Cor.11.16-12.10) and elsewhere (cf. II Cor.1.5; 13.4; Gal.6.17; Phil.1.20).

But now he speaks not only of this burden, of the oppression of suffering, of communion with the dead Lord, but also of the mysterious change in which death became life. He also experiences that in his bodily existence. Not only does God's power to endure work in his weakness, but even more that miraculous divine power which first in Jesus and subsequently again and again can create life out of suffering. Sufferings are like material which can be turned into its opposite. That is said in the same passage in II Corinthians with which we began and which may now be quoted as a whole:

But we have this treasure in earthen vessels, to show that the transcendent power belongs to God and not to us. We are afflicted in every way, but not crushed; perplexed, but not driven to despair; persecuted, but not forsaken; struck down, but not destroyed; always carrying around in the body the death of Jesus, so that the life of Jesus may also be manifested in our bodies. For while we live we are always being given up to death for Jesus' sake, so that the life of Jesus may be manifested in our mortal flesh (II Cor.4.7-11).

Certainly Paul is talking about himself and the service in which he has this experience. But he can probably talk in this way only because he is concerned with a basic experience of Christian existence which is accessible to everyone. Paul could put it in this way and did so. He had, though, to experience that association with Christ brings with it severe burdens, griefs, cares which otherwise would not have been heaped on him with such weight. The same law holds here: as dying, and behold we live – as poor yet making many rich – as having nothing, and yet possessing all things. Let us read the whole text:

We put no obstacle in anyone's way, so that no fault may be found with our ministry, but as servants of God we commend ourselves in every way: through great endurance, in afflictions, hardships, calamities, beatings, imprisonments, tumults, labours, watching, hunger; by purity, knowledge, forbearance, kindness, the Holy Spirit, genuine love, truthful speech, and the power of God; with the weapons of righteousness for the right hand and for the left; in honour and dishonour, in ill repute and good repute. We are treated as impostors, and yet as true; as unknown, and yet well known; as dying, and behold we live; as punished, and yet not killed; as sorrowful, yet always rejoicing: as poor, yet making many rich; as having nothing, and yet possessing everything (II Cor.6.3-10; cf.I Cor.4.9-13).

We might perhaps put it this way. The sufferings which there are in persevering in the service of Christ have remained like those which we met before: sickness, deprivation, hostility, maliciousness, humiliation and all the other things that are mentioned. But on the other hand they are not the same thing. They no longer lead to a diminution or even to annihilation. They can be seen and understood in quite a new way: as suffering, of the kind that Jesus also bore, indeed in truth as his suffering. We need not throw them out like evil intruders, hate them like the plague, defend ourselves against them as against robbers – however much deep down we may long to do this and often do. What is said here does not go against this normal human reaction to attacks of all kinds, far less can it be a general solution for the immeasurable and largely unrecompensed suffering of humanity. It is not a general statement about all kinds of threats to life and restrictions on life, but about those that arise as a result of service for Christ and a life directed towards him. In Paul it is the 'apostolic ministry' of which he says emphatically – amazingly enough – that he gives 'no one even the slightest offence' (II Cor.6.3), and that therefore there is no cause for all these hostilities and needs. Who of us could claim that? But what the apostle claims for himself is also open to others.

Despite the extent to which they have remained the 'old' ones, the sufferings have taken on a capacity for transformation for the one who understands himself to be in Christ. They have a part of the redemptive power which indwells the suffering of Christ; or to put it another way, they get into the field of force of the resurrection, by which the sufferings of Christ were already penetrated. Their negative nucleus can be changed into a positive charge. In them the apostle embraces Jesus himself who was killed. As he longs for communion with Jesus's suffering, he must not be surprised if that is what happens. Rather, he would need to be surprised were this not the case:

> That I may know Christ and the power of his resurrection, and may share his sufferings, becoming like him in his death (Phil.3.10).

The transformation happens all along the line. Poverty becomes riches, shame becomes true honour, weakness becomes strength. And what sounds most amazing: joy comes even out of his sufferings; in other words, something that would seem to be furthest removed from them and that those who afflicted him sought to prevent. 'As sorrowful, yet always rejoicing' (II Cor.6.10a; cf.7.4). Here perhaps it is most clear what opportunity is afforded by communion with his suffering: it is like a hidden glow which can be kindled to a bright flame and which burns the old material with it. We have in prospect even more than the hope for the glory that is prepared, for the future world, the longing to depart and be with Christ (Phil.1.23); we have an awareness that the present tribulation bears no relationship to the glory to come:

> I consider that the sufferings of this present time are not worth comparing with the glory that is to be revealed to us (Rom.8.18).

Or in a different way, in more compact language:

> For this slight momentary affliction is preparing for us an eternal weight of glory beyond all comparison, because we look not to the things that are seen but to the things that are unseen; for the things that are unseen are eternal (II Cor.4.17f.).

Now already, under the distressing, indeed often oppressive and desperate conditions of present circumstances, something may be experienced of the freedom to come – and particularly something to set against the dark and terrifying experiences which are diametrically opposed to it. More room would be needed for further reflection on this – a theme which can make up and occupy a whole life. Those who would have an inkling of this might be, for example, someone who does not want to count time spent in prison and blots it out of his life, or someone who sees a serious illness as a chance for reflection and a new start.

Besides, this transformation from black into white can be at work in the apostle for the benefit of more than the person concerned, in this case for him personally. Its fruit can also be exchanged for others which are useful to the community. Here there is a remarkable reciprocal relationship between apostle and community. The tribulations which he bears are a blessing for others because he accepted them in Christ and so they have been changed. Indeed the same thing could also happen the other way round, that what is laid on the community and borne by it also benefits the apostle: this is a community of giving and receiving in which an exchange of suffering and mutual comfort comes into being.

There is specific mention of comfort and giving comfort at the beginning of II Corinthians. Certainly this is no cheap comfort as in conventional 'words of comfort', nor an easy comfort, as with the tears of children which dry quickly. Nor does it come from human compassion or even the power and tenderness of one's own heart. Here comfort is the gift of God, the raising up of those who have been completely laid low, encouragement to go on, peace from God's heart. In parallel to the suffering of Christ we could also speak of the comfort of Christ. Such comfort goes to and fro, between apostle and community, as through a piped system, from the 'fellowship with his suffering':

> Blessed be the God and Father of our Lord Jesus Christ, the Father of mercies and God of all comfort, who comforts us in all our affliction, so that we may be able to comfort those who are in any affliction, with the comfort with which we ourselves are comforted by God. For as we share abundantly in Christ's sufferings, so through Christ we share abundantly in comfort too. If we are afflicted, it is for your comfort and salvation; and if we are comforted, it is for your comfort, which you experience when you patiently endure the same sufferings that we suffer. Our hope for you is unshaken; for we know that as you share in our sufferings you will also share in our comfort (II Cor.1.3-7; cf. also 7.4; 8.1f.; 13.9).

Thus the apostle can become a teacher not only of faith but also of life 'in Christ'; for some perhaps a teacher second to none. That these last insights are not fantasy, mystification or falsification of our sorry condition is shown by those who have followed this course. One thinks of the early martyrs, who went triumphantly to death and held the trembling hands of their executioners (the martyrdom of Felicitas and Perpetua); the English Lord Chancellor Thomas More who pushed aside his beard on the block with the wry comment that it had done no evil; down to those who were the victims of 20 July 1944 and indeed Jews who could utter moving prayers – even for forgiveness – in concentration camps. This dimension of human life, through suffering into victory and indeed joy, is accessible to anyone who is open to it. Paul resolutely interpreted it in the light of Christ and was able to experience its truth in his person. 'Power is made perfect in weakness.'

NOTES

1. Fridolin Stier, *Vielleicht ist irgendwo Tag*, Freiburg 1981, 18f.
2. Günther Bornkamm, *Paul*, Hodder and Stoughton and Harper and Row 1971.
3. For this I would refer to my teacher, Professor F.W.Meier, and the lectures which I heard in Munich between 1947 and 1951.
4. For instance one of my older colleagues said that some years ago he had difficulty in getting the Imprimatur from the episcopal authorities for the prayer that the Lord should purify his church from 'all stains and impurities'. The church was utterly pure!
5. At this point I must at least draw attention to the fact that this very brief description of the relationship between Jesus and the New Testament writers indicates my own theological conviction which is also shared by many other New Testament scholars, but that it does not represent a universal viewpoint.
6. A. Deissmann, *St Paul. A Study in Social and Religious History*, Hodder and Stoughton ²1926, 59.
7. The expression 'Jewish Christianity' intrinsically denotes only the origin of believers. They come from Judaism and are therefore circumcised, and moulded by the tradition of Old Testament Jewish faith, in contrast to those who came to believe as pagans; these were then described with the collective term 'Gentile Christians'.
8. There is a detailed account in G.Dautzenberg, *Urchristliche Prophetie*, BWANT 104, Stuttgart 1975, 257-73.
9. Cf. the voices of those who hate Paul including P. de Lagarde and F.Nietzsche, etc., in Bornkamm, *Paul*, 230-4; H.J.Schoeps, *Paul. The Theology of the Apostle in the Light of Jewish Religious History*, Lutterworth Press 1961, 262-80.
10. From *Stundenbuch*, Einsiedeln, etc., 1978ff., Lectionary I/4, pp.10f., middle.
11. N.Schneider, *Die rhetorische Eigenart der paulinischen Antithese*, Tübingen 1970, 19.
12. If we are to understand these different kinds of account in Acts we should be aware that a favourite method in ancient historiography was to explain important events by speeches and to construct these speeches quite freely. The author of Acts also made use of this method abundantly and in sovereign fashion, above all in the cases of Peter and Paul.
13. We cannot know for certain exactly what Paul meant by 'thorn in the flesh' and 'messenger of Satan'. A severe illness? The burden of his stressful life? A hereditary affliction? We do not know and can only guess.

14. In themselves, 'eschatological', 'eschatology', simply mean 'of the end time', 'doctrine of the end time'. It is hard to do without the terms in theology, which is why I use them often here. However, the terminology fluctuates over quite a wide range.

15. Only once does he put the periods of Abraham and Moses in chronological order, in Gal.3.15-25 (cf.Rom.4). But even there the orientation in terms of content on the contrast between promise and law is predominant. The promise is older than the law and has better credentials.

16. Cf. M.Hengel, *Crucifixion*, SCM Press and Fortress Press 1977.

17. H.Schlier, *Der Römerbrief*, Freiburg 1977, 48.

18. E.Käsemann, 'The Saving Significance of the Death of Jesus in Paul', in *Perspectives on Paul*, SCM Press and Fortress Press 1971, 32-59 (43).

19. For those who want to look up the passages I list them here: Rom.4.24f.; 6.4,9; 7.4; (8.11); 8.34; 10.9; I Cor.6.14; 15.4,12,13,14,15,16,17,20; II Cor.4.14; 5.15; Gal.1.1; I Thess.1.10. For questions connected with the resurrection of Jesus see U.Wilckens, *Resurrection*, St Andrew Press 1978.

20. I cannot give further arguments for that here. But it should at least be noted as food for thought and for the reader's own observation.

21. The only comparable, but not exact occurrences, would be those in II Cor.13.4; Phil.2.8; a different view is to be taken of the term 'crucified with' in Gal.2.19; Rom.6.6; the formalistic mention of the cross in the Deutero-Paulines, Col.1.20; 2.14; Eph.2.16, is clearly different.

22. This is what Käsemann says in the article mentioned in n.18 using a saying of Luther, *crux sola est nostra theologia* (the cross alone is our theology), which Käsemann, however, makes the canon for a forced interpretation of Paul (pp.48, 50, 54, 58, cf. 59): 'Here (viz. in Paul) the theology of the resurrection is a chapter in the theology of the cross, not the excelling of it. Since Paul, all theological controversy has radiated ultimately from one central point and hence can only be decided at that point: *crux sola nostra theologia.*'

23. I simply list a few passages that the reader can look up: Rom.5.8f.: 6.3f., 8,9,10; 8.13,34; I Cor.15.22; I Thess.4.14.

24. Cf.K.Kertelge, *Rechtfertigung bei Paulus*, NTA 3, Münster 1967, 28-33.

25. For the first orientation cf. e.g. F.Nötscher and P.Bläser, 'Gerechtigkeit',in J.B.Bauer (ed.), *Bibeltheologisches Wörterbuch* I, Graz ²1962, 452-73.

26. A remarkable idea which in addition to this passage, Gal.3.17, also appears as an invitation in Rom.13.14.

27. Cf. e.g. I Cor.11.2-16. Moreover, Paul is neither a misogynist nor one who despises marriage; but we cannot go into that here since it would take us too far afield; cf. e.g. H.Baltensweiler, *Die Ehe im Neuen Testament*, Zurich and Stuttgart 1967, and the abundance of literature which followed it, in H.Schürmann, 'Neutestamentliche Marginalien zur Frage nach der Institutionalität, Unauflosbarkeit und Sakramentalität der Ehe', in *Kirche und Bibel*, FS E.Schick, Paderborn 1979, 409-30.

28. Nevertheless the apostle struggles painfully to be able to maintain the priority of the calling of Israel despite the rejection that it has shown: Rom.9-11.

29. Glossolalia (speaking with tongues) is an ecstatic but inarticulate form of speech that also appears outside the Christian sphere, which in the community in

Corinth gave rise to tensions and dispute. Paul attempts to get a grip on the disorder which has arisen in worship.